Experience in Action!

DesignBuild in Architecture

Experience in Action!
DesignBuild in Architecture

Vera Simone Bader and Andres Lepik (Ed.)

Edition **DETAIL**

A.M.

PROJECTS

Preface

ANDRES LEPIK

The study of architecture is essentially based on the acquisition of abstract knowledge through subjects such as structural analysis, building physics, history, theory, construction law, etc. Furthermore, design is conveyed with a focus on plans and sections, facade views, digital renderings, and models, which are left without the prospect of actual execution. In most cases, students only get to put their skills into practice after graduation, and even once they have joined an architectural practice, it still takes a long time before they can experience a full project from design to handover of the construction. In contrast to the field of medicine, in which students have contact with patients early on, giving them an impression of the immediate impact of their discipline, architectural studies do not facilitate much direct contact with the reality of building, such as the handling of material, inclusion of context, dialogue with craftspersons, as well as with the expectations and demands of the future users.

This is why a number of universities have expanded their curricula with DesignBuild programs, in an effort to bridge the gap between abstract knowledge and concrete experience. During these programs, students plan actual building projects and build them as a team. Such DesignBuild programs, which were relatively scarce before – forerunners being Yale University back in 1967 or Rural Studio in Alabama since 1993 – are recently enjoying increasing popularity at universities. On the one hand, this seems to be due to the fact that many lecturers want to close the gap between the acquisition of abstract knowledge and actual application. On the other hand, it often appears to be due to a rising demand for them by students. Essential factors for the increasing demand include direct experience of craftsmanship, teamwork, and not least, the social aspect of the built projects. The students plan and build kindergartens, schools, meeting places for refugees, or living spaces for people in need and thereby gain hands-on insight into the social dimension of their discipline. DesignBuild programs provide a useful instrument for the "social turn" of architecture, helping to develop an awareness for the ethical dimension of the profession during the education phase.

DesignBuild programs offers – in the United States, Europe, and meanwhile also in Asia – have increased in recent years, resulting in a flood of publications on individual projects and on the programs of individual schools. A website (dbxchange.eu) aims to provide a communal platform for the exchange of knowledge and experience between participants. Academic consideration of the DesignBuild movement and its historical-theoretical classification is still in its early stages, however. This may be because there is neither a binding definition of what DesignBuild exactly entails and what it is supposed to achieve, nor a valid methodology. Additionally lacking is a systematic approach to historical aspects and guidelines to evaluate completed projects. It is in the nature of most DesignBuild initiatives to build on the idealism of those involved, namely that of the lecturers and students, but often also of the respective partners on location. This means that all of the energy during planning and execution goes into realization – and not into theoretical consideration and reflective observation. The increasing number of programs, however, also gives rise to more and more critical voices: For example, doesn't the fact that teachers and students from industrialized countries are traveling to developing countries to realize social projects there have a neocolonialist tinge?

The exhibition and accompanying catalogue "Experience in Action!" present a comparison of 16 examples of DesignBuild programs and set the foundations for deeper reflection and debate. The Architecture Museum of TUM is a suitable place for this. Firstly, because the Chair of Hermann Kaufmann at our Faculty of Architecture has successfully offered a range of DesignBuild programs since 2007, which has led to the realization of numerous national and international projects. Secondly, because we have already touched upon the DesignBuild topic several times in our exhibition program. With "Experience in Action!" we want to provide a focused presentation of DesignBuild as a teaching method. We strongly believe that DesignBuild should be not an optional offer but rather a fixed component of the education of the next generation of architects. In order to strengthen the interdisciplinary orientation of the programs, we also aim to incorporate further aspects of ethics, psychology, and sociology in the DesignBuild discussion. Global society will likely face extreme challenges in the era we live in. The field of architecture should therefore adapt as soon as possible in order to prove its social relevance. DesignBuild is a good start.

Experience in Action! On the Development of the DesignBuild Method

VERA SIMONE BADER

DesignBuild refers to a teaching method used at various schools of architecture since the beginning of the modern age, which has gained worldwide recognition especially over the past two decades. The term originates from the building industry and describes a project delivery system, and hence a "process, in which the realization of a building from conceptual development and design to execution are in one hand."[1] Some lecturers, however, consider this definition to be too narrow, since it encompasses the process but not the social aspect immanent in these projects. In architecture, the term first appeared in 1971 in connection with the Design and Construction program at Goddard College in the USA, which was led by the American architect David Sellers.[2] Alternative terms such as "1to1," "social design," "hands on," etc. are therefore often used.[3] So far, the term DesignBuild has not become fully accepted in architectural discourse. One questionable aspect is the emphasis on the planners' obligation to deliver a finished building. In fact, nearly all the DesignBuild projects initiated at schools of architecture aim to fulfil this obligation towards the clients and users – be it through permanent buildings or temporary installations. The risk here is of underestimating that this is a teaching method at university level, and therefore involves much more than the execution of a project.

So, what are the general issues regarding DesignBuild projects today? Certainly, one key aspect is learning a design method that can be adapted to given economic, ecological, social, and functional conditions, as well as gaining a new horizon of experience through instruction in independent building. Moreover, students are expected to develop a feeling for the implementation of architectural ideas. The realization of a spatial program alone is not enough; the projects must have an aesthetic expression. This is one of the biggest challenges, precisely because the projects are carried out with little money, locally available materials, and by budding architects. Sacrificing aesthetic qualities is not an option, however. They form a fundamental requirement because they also demonstrate the projects' future relevance. And apart from that? Perhaps the inclusion of methods and facts from different disciplines, which are useful for understanding and categorizing complex, dissonant situations as well as for questioning one's own position and practice. After all, reflecting on the what and why and for whom the students are doing a project is just as much part of the task that motivates them to think and act independently. In an ideal case, DesignBuild includes critical analysis of the task itself. Students may be happy to see their designs realized – yet longer-term effects for both students and users are not always clearly evident. Ultimately, this also means that projects should be evaluated as a whole and that evaluations of their processes must be designed for the long term.

◀◀
Operating building for a hospital in Ngaoubela, Cameroon, TUM, 2012

◀
Richard Buckminster Fuller and his students hanging on the geodesic dome they built, 1948

The reason for a lack of sustainability should be attributed less to the lecturers and rather to an often non-existent anchorage of the DesignBuild projects at the universities. Most of the institutions have established neither a platform nor a professorial chair for this urgently needed form of exchange, making it very difficult to build up a pool of experience through fixed-term academic staff. The projects are moreover subordinate to the conventional curriculum of the faculties, leaving no time for equally important aspects such as research, analysis, and evaluation. Three educational institutions of the past demonstrate how such an integration can be achieved more successfully – Bauhaus in Germany, Black Mountain College in the USA, and Ciudad Abierta (Open City) in Chile. In contrast to other architectural schools, all three of these establishments tested radical pedagogical measures, making them particularly suitable examples of an integral approach, together with relevant learning objectives. This teaching approach, now known as the DesignBuild method has always been part of their program – and moreover has contributed to a profound reflection on the schools' indivudal approach.

Participatory and interdisciplinary work: Bauhaus

The exhibition building at the end of Am Horn Street, built at Bauhaus Weimar in 1924 under the direction of Walter Gropius, is one of the earliest examples of the DesignBuild method and frequently cited as a reference.[4] The painter Georg Muche, the youngest master at the Bauhaus, won an internal competition at the school with his design. Building management, however, had to be assumed by Gropius's construction office, since the school had no architectural class at the time.[5] The construction was carried out by Soziale Bauhütte Weimar. Nevertheless, all the Bauhaus workshops participated in furnishing and design, so that the building became a demonstration of the program at the internationally influential school and the interaction of theory and practice. A tiered curriculum offered the necessary prerequisites, allowing students to encounter different materials early and learn how to use them during their basic training, before testing their skills at the design studio and in building practice.[6]

After the move to Dessau one year later, Gropius set up an architecture department with the idea of embedding the practical construction experiences in the Bauhaus curriculum; the idea was finally implemented by his successor.[7] Hannes Meyer expanded the architecture curriculum with the objective of realizing his fundamental ideas on communal building, the so-called co-op principle. The focus was less on design as an aesthetic process, while studies to determine requirements became more important instead. Scientific analyses were to be carried out in advance, such as the documentation of daily routines and ecological conditions.[8] To a certain extent, students used empirical research methods from the social sciences to determine the needs of people. The observations were then to be incorporated in the designs. Philipp Tolziner, a mural painting and architecture student, commented on this rather critically, however, writing that "the method of project planning taught in building theory and applied in the architecture studio [remained] the same as before [after all]."[9] Nevertheless, Meyer undoubtedly promoted an interdisciplinary approach, also by inviting academics from other areas such as philosophy, ethics,

"Laubenganghäuser" (multifamily houses with balcony access) in Dessau-Törten, built by Bauhaus students under the direction of Hannes Meyer, 1929–1930

psychology, sociology, and urban planning to lectures at the Bauhaus. They were to examine the architectural design and building process from all aspects and promote the students' awareness of the many different perspectives and factors to be taken into account in their designs.[10]

Meyer thus focused on an integral approach, which also involved the students working together during the design and construction processes. Again and again, Meyer attempted to initiate practical building projects, but often failed due to lack of financing or for construction law reasons.[11] Despite the difficult initial situation, many Bauhaus students still managed to realize their designs. Particularly noteworthy in this context was the expansion of the Dessau-Törten housing estate initiated by Gropius with the construction of Laubenganghäuser (multifamily houses with balcony access).

So-called vertical brigades were utilized for the design and construction of the social housing, which required students at all training levels to cooperate and give up authorship on account of the collaborative process.[12] These projects were fully in line with Meyer's teaching, promoting self-responsibility as well as interdisciplinary and participatory thinking.

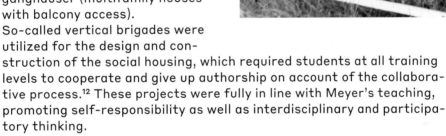

Anti-hierarchical and experimental thinking: Black Mountain College

Black Mountain College, strongly influenced by Bauhaus and established near Asheville, North Carolina in 1933, used practical building activities as a teaching method for entirely different goals.[13] John Andrew Rice, its founder and first rector, wanted to create a progressive educational institution that focused on every individual's creativity. In contrast to other universities, it provided training not only for architects and artists, but also for mathematicians, actors, and natural scientists. Inspired by the educational reformer John Dewey, Rice developed a curriculum founded on learning by doing; on observation and experimentation.[14]

In an interview, Rice outlined the philosophical underpinnings of the curriculum as follows: "In the meantime, our central and consistently practiced approach consists of teaching methods rather than contents; putting emphasis on the process and not on the result; making students realize that their handling of the facts and themselves in the midst of the facts has become more important than the facts themselves. Because facts change, but the method of handling them – provided it is the free, dynamic method of life itself – remains the same."[15] Therefore an open-ended, problem-oriented approach was taught, rather than conveying prefabricated knowledge with fixed realities.

The most famous example for this type of training is the project initiated by Richard Buckminster Fuller for the summer school in 1948.[16] Together with his students, he worked on the construction of a geodesic dome.

Richard Buckminster Fuller (left), Josef Albers (right) and the students erect the geodesic dome, 1948

The experimental building, which represented the house of the future for Fuller, collapsed immediately after completion. Fuller didn't take this initial failure too seriously though: he said that 90 % of avant-garde work consisted of failure.[17] With their newly gained experience, the students managed to successfully construct the building in a second attempt. The work program played an overall central role at the college: students and professors, men and women alike, were responsible for the structural maintenance of the farm and administrative buildings.[18] It was all about designing the day-to-day world as an action-oriented social practice. Designing and building together was supposed to strengthen the anti-authoritarian sense of community and convey a deeper understanding of democratic ideals. This also included students and teachers living together and sharing meals at Black Mountain College, in order to encounter each other as members of equal rank in a social unit. The intention was to dissolve the boundaries of role distribution between teachers and students; between those directing and those acting.[19] The biggest project developed at Black Mountain College in less than two years was the Studies Building, a two-storey, 30-metre-long building with more than 60 workspaces for students, studios for teachers, as well as several common rooms. The design originated from Lawrence Kocher, who taught as a professor at the college, but all the work was coordinated and carried out by the students and lecturers with the support of a few local craftsmen. The college deliberately crossed the boundaries of traditional experience processes, in order to sound out new, transformational practices.

Radically different: Ciudad Abierta

Some pedagogic practices based on the DesignBuild method were even more liberal. In the mid-1950s, several professors, architects, and artists around the Chilean architect Alberto Cruz and the Argentinian poet Godofredo Iommi Marini traveled through South America in a performative act and embarked on a communal quest for identity and alternatives to the conventional understanding of architecture.[20] They attempted to explore new forms of modernism through spontaneous performances and poetry. The interaction of poetry and architecture was particularly important here: the vague, immanent, and ephemeral were to be given shape, and words, contents, and interpretation were to be transferred to an architectural space. Furthermore, intensive interaction with the immediate surroundings became a key focus: topography, light conditions, and materiality were sketched, sculptures and installations were improvised. The goal was to make a stand against the functionality, technical modernization and utopian social programs tied to the ideas of modernism in Europe and the United States. The focus was on radical experimentation and the opposition of colonial ideas as well as institutional, bureaucratic, and capitalist structures. Neither social commitment nor political ideas played a role here, however – not even after the coup d'état by Augusto Pinochet.[21] Instead, the followers tested other production forms of architecture that counteracted the usual interrelationships. A few years later, these ideas became tied to a place: the construction of Ciudad Abierta (Open City) started in 1971. It was established in a sandy area on the Pacific Coast, in Ritoque near Valparaiso. The remote site is used for educational and architectural experiments to this day. Students, professors, and artists live in and work together on houses, pavilions, and sculptures spread around the 275-hectare terrain. They are occupied partly by professors and partly by guests and used for performances and readings. The pedagogical practice here again serves to remove the boundaries between learning, working, and living.[22] The focus is on rethinking architecture by combining it with poetry and physical activities. This is intended to help find an individual connection to South

American architecture and art. The DesignBuild method therefore forms part of an entirely divergent creative process, which integrates completely different ways of artistic thinking.

Learning to learn

In the past, DesignBuild projects as activist interventions were often part of large-scale pedagogical experiments that significantly advanced the discourse and practice of architecture.[23] Traditional foundations and methods of architectural education were to be overcome; questioning normative thinking was to generate the energy to create space for new architectural ideas. To this end, traditional roles of academic teaching were also given up. Today, these activist confrontations are increasingly demanded by students who do not want to passively stand by and watch the rapid changes in the world. The DesignBuild method presents this precise opportunity of incorporating experimental practices as a learning and teaching method into critical architectural thinking and acting. This implies that possible learning outcomes of this method must also include interdisciplinary research, the application of participatory strategies, an anti-hierarchical, democratic, and experimental way of thinking, and an openness to diverse creative processes. The fact that they are in demand is illustrated by the student interviews in this catalogue, but also by the texts of the authors focusing on current topics such as participation, evaluation, and cultural aspects and providing a differentiated consideration of the status of this teaching method today. The goal is to represent the current state of the discussion using fundamental aspects as well as to raise new questions. After all, due to its experimental nature, DesignBuild is by no means a static, but a constantly developing method.

Experimental education and games at the architecture faculty in Chile

Exhibition and catalogue

Given the increasingly large number of initiatives involving the DesignBuild method, it has become almost impossible to map out a complete overview of the current situation anymore. Matters are made even more difficult by the fact that many initiatives, especially from South America and Asia, are hard to locate, despite websites such as dbxchange.eu that aim to establish a network. The exhibition "Experience in Action! DesignBuild in Architecture" and the associated catalogue can therefore only provide a stimulus for a deeper consideration of the meaning, necessity, and forms of implementation of this teaching method. For this purpose, 16 specific projects from Germany and abroad are presented. The examples consist chiefly of projects aiming to result in complete and permanent buildings, since the prerequisites – regarding the handling of users alone – vary greatly for temporary installations. The selection includes different construction tasks such as residential houses, theaters, schools, kindergartens, and hospitals that have been built in the geographical neighborhood of the respective school of architecture or in underdeveloped regions. Moreover, projects initiated by universities and lecturers with a significant wealth of experience were principally taken into account. The presented examples are divided into four categories, representing the entire process that the projects go through: research, dialogue, design, and the actual building phase. The focus is more on a consideration of the process than on the finished object. This serves to demonstrate the different focus areas and goals of the DesignBuild method, as well as the strong social commitment of the students and lecturers. The powerful motivation that drives them, especially in the light of the increasing challenges for global society, can continue to be considered a future-oriented approach to architecture.

1 https://www.code.tu-berlin.de/design-build.php (accessed 30 January 2020).

2 Tolya Stonorov, Danny Sagan, "Time Map: Graphic History of the Academic Design-Build Studio Case Studies," in: Tolya Stonorov (ed.), *The Design-Build Studio. Crafting Meaningful Work in Architecture Education,* New York 2018, pp. 6–16.

3 Since the term DesignBuild has become more and more established in the respective publications in recent years, it shall also be used throughout this catalogue.

4 Branislav Folić, Saja Kosanović, Tadej Glažar, Alenka Fikfak, *Design-Build Concept in Architectural Education,* in: https://www.degruyter.com/downloadpdf/j/aup.2016.11.issue-1/aup-2016-0007/aup-2016-0007.pdf.

5 Anke Blümm, "Bauentwurf, Bauausführung und Ausstattung," in: Martina Ullrich (ed.): *Haus am Horn. Bauhaus-Architektur in Weimar,* Weimar 2019, pp. 80–87, here pp. 81f.

6 Klaus-Jürgen Winkler, *Baulehre und Entwerfen am Bauhaus. 1919–1933,* Weimar 2003.

7 Anne Stengel, "Architekturlehre und Praxisbezug unter Hannes Meyer am Bauhaus Dessau 1928 bis 1930," in: Carola Eber, Eva Maria Froschauer, Christiane Salge (eds.), *Vom Baumeister zum Master. Formen der Architekturlehre vom 19. bis ins 21. Jahrhundert,* Berlin 2019, pp. 104–121, here p. 105. The students mainly completed building internships in Gropius's private office.

8 Anne Stengel, "Baupraxis als Lehre," in: Philipp Oswald (ed.), *Hannes Meyers neue Bauhauslehre. Von Dessau bis Mexiko,* Berlin 2019, pp. 130–142.

9 "Philipp Tolziner, Student der Wandmalerei und Bauabteilung (1927–30)," in: Philipp Oswald (ed.), *Hannes Meyers neue Bauhauslehre. Von Dessau bis Mexiko,* Berlin 2019, p. 111.

10 Hannes Meyer was clearly influenced by the texts of the pedagogue and philosopher Johann Heinrich Pestalozzi. Anne Stengel, "Architekturlehre und Praxisbezug unter Hannes Meyer am Bauhaus Dessau 1928 bis 1930," in: *Vom Baumeister zum Master,* pp. 104–121, here pp. 110f.

11 Ibid., pp. 112f.

12 Hilde Strobl, "Hannes Meyer – Co-op. Architektur als soziales Gestaltungsprinzip," in: Sandra Hofmeister (ed.) *Our Bauhaus Heritage,* Munich 2019, p. 71.

13 Fabienne Eggelhöfer, "Was am Bauhaus und am Black Mountain College gelehrt wurde," in: Egon Blume et al. (eds.): *Black Mountain. Ein interdisziplinäres Experiment 1933–1957,* exhibition catalogue Hamburger Bahnhof, Leipzig 2015, pp. 110–119.

14 John Dewey is considered as an essential founder of this method and already used the term in his texts *Schools of Tomorrow* (1900) and *Democracy and Education* (1916).

15 Louis Adamic, "Education on a Mountain," in: *Harper's Magazine,* April 1936.

16 Eva Diaz, *The Experimenters: Chance and Design at Black Mountain College,* Chicago 2015, pp. 101–149.

17 Craig Schuftan, *Alternativer Staat,* in: *Black Mountain. Ein interdisziplinäres Experiment 1933–1957,* p. 430.

18 Matilda Felix, *Constructing Experience. Architektur am Black Mountain College,* pp. 196–239, here p. 232.

19 Ibid., p. 197.

20 Ignacio Gonzalez Galan, "A Pursuit for a 'Change of Life:' Pedagogical Experiences, Poetic Occupations and Historical Frictions," in: Sony Devabhaktuni, Patricia Guaita and Cornelia Tapparelli (eds.), *Building Cultures Valparaiso: Pedagogy, Practice and Poetry at the Valparaiso School of Architecture and Design,* Lausanne 2015.

21 Ana Maria Léon, "Prisoners of Ritoque: The Open City and the Ritoque Concentration Camp," in: *Journal of Architectural Education,* Massachusetts Institute of Technology, 2012: https://www.academia.edu/5361441/Prisoners_of_Ritoque_The_Open_City_and_the_Ritoque_Concentration_Camp.

22 Agnes Dransfeld, "Ciudad Abierta in Ritoque," in: *Bauwelt,* No. 3, 2015.

23 Beatriz Colomina, Ignazio Gonzalez Galan, Evangelos Kotsioris and Anna-Maria Meister, "Radical Pedagogies: Notes Towards a Taxonomy of Global Experiments," in: Sony Devabhaktuni, Patricia Guaita, Cornelia Tapparelli (eds.), *Building Cultures Valparaiso: Pedagogy, Practice and Poetry at the Valparaiso School of Architecture and Design,* Lausanne 2015.

24 Beatriz Colomina, "Auf dem Weg zu einer radikalen Pädagogik," in: *Baunetzwoche,* No. 539: https://www.baunetz.de/baunetzwoche/baunetzwoche_ausgabe_6932906.html.

There is No Right Building in the Wrong One – DesignBuild as Opportunity and Risk

MARTIN DÜCHS

The philosopher Theodor W. Adorno once said: "There is no right life in the wrong one."[1] This is undoubtedly one of the most cited philosophical sentences in the eternal list of best quotes. The degree of familiarity is in fact so large that the sentence has developed a certain life of its own, occasionally distancing itself a little from its author, and certainly far from its context. This context is of particular interest to architects. With his apodictic conclusion, Adorno in fact summarized a short reflection reproduced in *Minima Moralia* under the heading "Refuge for the Homeless" ("Asyl für Obdachlose"). The same title could also be assumed to refer to a DesignBuild project. The teaching method has become increasingly popular in the education of architects, thanks to the added didactic value it offers in terms of the practical realization of projects compared to theoretical designs, but also due to its emphatic social character.[2] Put bluntly, it's about actually doing something and helping in the process. A moral-philosophical[3] assessment of Design-Build as a didactic approach in the teaching of architecture could therefore be expected to have an entirely positive outcome – no more hot air or plans created for the shredder, and doing something good at the same time. In the following, I will attempt to show that DesignBuild is certainly a positive opportunity for students in the manner indicated, but that it also poses a risk due to the social as well as practical character of the teaching method. In order to take advantage of the opportunity, while confronting this risk at the same time, it is paradoxically necessary to subject this practically oriented approach to in-depth theoretical scrutiny, as well as place the concrete social aspect in a larger context. Otherwise one could possibly end up with a potentially right building in a wrong one.

DesignBuild – opportunity and risk

Despite their diversity, DesignBuild projects exhibit two main characteristics. For one, practice and a hands-on approach are in the foreground. The approach is based on the assumption that focus on practice

◀◀
Experimental building in the Ciudad Abierta

◀
The Adorno monument on the university campus in Frankfurt, 2016

and emphasis of the entirety of the architectural genesis process from design to completed constructions[4] is associated with added educational value, which consists of learning and practicing many hard and soft skills. The emphasis on hands-on is attended by a degree of scepticism towards teaching that remains stuck in theory and intellectual conceptualization or theorizing. An architectural trend that has generally been observed since the 1980s is reflected here on a small scale in architectural teaching, namely a turning away from an architecture characterized by ideas and an intellectual approach, to one focusing on the concrete sensory perception of space and materials.[5]

Secondly, social motivation is recognizable in almost all DesignBuild projects. The point is not to create nice little aesthetic showpieces, but to use architectural interventions for social impact. This can range from isolated aids for specific socially disadvantaged groups to buildings or interventions intended to improve the cohesion of an entire (urban) society.[6] This characteristic also reflects a large-scale development, namely a desire that started in the late 1990s, to increasingly re-emphasize the social role of architecture away from aestheticization and "architecture of neoliberalism."[7] The motto of the Venice Biennale's 7th International Architecture Exhibition in 2000, curated by Massimiliano Fuksas, can be quoted paradigmatically in this context: "Less Aesthetics, More Ethics!"[8]

DesignBuild is therefore supposed to kill two birds with one stone, as it were. An educational goal is to be pursued with the emphasis on a hands-on approach on the one hand, while the intention is generally to improve the world a little on the other – or with reference to Adorno and the borrowed title: using right building to make life a little less wrong. The outcome of an intuitive moral evaluation must be positive in the light of such goals. Yet, on closer inspection and taking into account ethics, some aspects could be considered questionable. This particularly applies to DesignBuild projects that are within the broad context of development assistance programs. Two specific issues that clearly arise in this regard are neocolonial perspectives and the sustainability of the aid given. To avoid confronting such perfectly legitimate reservations, many DesignBuild projects prefer to deal with problems in the immediate neighborhood and attempt to improve social deficits in the students' home city. This additionally meets the desired objective of gaining a better understanding of the building process and relevant actors in the students' own country. Students furthermore have an opportunity to gain experience regarding the social impact of their own actions and to acquire knowhow related to the building realization process in the environment of their home city.

Are national DesignBuild projects therefore entirely positive from an ethics perspective? Unfortunately this cannot be claimed per se either, because the approach bears two hazards. The first is to understand architecture as morally relevant only when social projects are involved. Solely the pursuit of social objectives in architecture would be understood as "moral" or "ethical building" or "ethics in architecture." This is however wrong in terms of terminology and content, and implies a dangerous restriction of the morally relevant aspects of architecture.[9] The second risk is that emphasis on the practical character of DesignBuild may lead to a generally negative view of a theoretical consideration of architecture as well as to a questioning of its use.

Note from the Welfare Bureau for the Transcendentally Homeless

The first risk mentioned has to do with the philosophical dimension of architecture. Adorno's text mentioned at the beginning commences with a version of the conclusion, namely the statement that "actually one

can no longer dwell any longer" today (the book was first published in 1951).[10] With this, he opposes traditional bourgeois apartments on the one hand, but also modern apartments committed to socialist ideas on the other. The latter he refers to as "cases made by technical experts for philistines, or factory sites which have strayed into the sphere of consumption, without any relation to the dweller."[11] Neither here nor there does Adorno find it possible to dwell: "From a distance, the difference between Vienna Workshop and Bauhaus becomes less significant."[12] This gives the term dwelling a far-reaching meaning, endowing architecture and the architect with a great moral responsibility. For Adorno, dwelling not only means staying in one's own apartment, but being-in-the-world in a manner appropriate for a person as a human being. Hence, he is concerned about a being-at-home in a broad sense, which is now no longer possible in general, since human beings have become "transcendentally homeless" in a modern society shaped by capitalism or fascism.[13] Martin Heidegger takes the same line in 1952, a time in which Germany was still far from being able to provide even close to satisfactory housing[14] conditions for everyone, when he characterizes the existential homelessness of people as being a much bigger problem compared to the general shortage of housing. Correspondingly, the "ethical function of architecture" extends far beyond fighting social shortcomings.[15] Architecture must aim to remove the existential homelessness or Adorno's transcendental homelessness of human beings.

DesignBuild projects are contrary to this aim when architecture students and their lecturers want to help in practice, in the sense of "ethical architecture" and – possibly – fail to understand the existential dimension of architecture and, at worst, ignore it in their later professional life. This would make DesignBuild projects a mere moral fig leaf and a feel-good pill for one's own conscience, with an effect destined to be forgotten already by the next semester.

However, if DesignBuild projects help students to understand the existential significance of architecture beyond the immediate phase of social assistance, its ethical function, and hence their immense moral responsibility as architects, then they can be an important component of architectural teaching. It is imperative to clarify that architecture is a morally, highly relevant activity, not only in social projects, but always,

Summer school at the Multihalle Mannheim: living experiments as models of an open society, 2019

and that architects correspondingly carry great moral responsibility in their work irrespective of specific projects. The fact that a well-known network of DesignBuild programs bears the title Home not Shelter!, however, indicates that this aspect has found its way into the fundamental understanding of the approach.[16]

Theory is dead! Long live theory!

The second problem associated with DesignBuild is that students may regard a theoretical consideration of their work as architects as unnecessary because the "form of cognition derived from doing" ("Erkenntnisform, die aus dem machen entsteht")[17] is superior to any theorizing. This is however fundamentally flawed: improvement of a given situation is the aim of every architectural project, not only of DesignBuild projects. In order to be able to assess whether an improvement has been made, a measure is required. In as far as architecture shapes the lives of people in an extensive manner, this measure will be – implicitly or explicitly – that of a good life. The ideal of a good life is however neither given, nor self-evident or unequivocal. This is particularly applicable against the background of an increasingly differentiated and diversified society. The measure of a good life should therefore be justified rationally and defined deliberately, because intuitive justification strategies have lost their authority in view of the mentioned heterogeneity and complexity of social reality. Models of a good life must be justified if there is no longer a consensus on them. In as far as architecture ultimately aims to facilitate a good life, architects must consider eudemonistic aspects systematically. This means that a theoretical reflection regarding objectives and methods is more necessary than ever in architecture. Just doing is simply not enough any longer.[18]

What follows: DesignBuild as right learning in the wrong learning?

A moral-philosophical evaluation of DesignBuild leads to a paradoxical conclusion: precisely this practice-oriented method needs solid theoretical supplementation in order to meet the problematic aspects referred to. From a didactic perspective, a lack of theoretical classification and foundation firstly poses the risk that DesignBuild projects serve as moral fig leaves or, going back to Adorno's sentence: one may be building right once, but will not gain the right view of the moral character of the work of an architect and the associated responsibility. By and large, one will therefore remain in the wrong mindset. The second thing potentially happening is that students simply do not see the fundamental necessity of theoretical reflection in the architectural profession. In other words: if just-simply-doing is the most important thing, then the fact that one should question the meaning behind what one is just simply doing may get left behind. As a practice-oriented teaching method, DesignBuild therefore requires in-depth theoretical support.

What else remains to be said about the DesignBuild method? There may be no right life in the wrong one but, from an ethical point of view, at least a right building. This is one that tries to provide a home for people in a physical but also in a transcendental sense and to let people dwell despite all the problems of their time. DesignBuild can help to sensitize future architects for this goal. The method can, however, also lead students to blindly doing things for the sake of doing and hence make them insensitive to the actual ethical function of architecture. The result of the ethical assessment of DesignBuild is therefore clearly ambiguous: it depends.

Martin Düchs studied architecture and philosophy in Munich, Paris, and Gothenburg.
After obtaining his Diplom (German university degree), he worked as an architect for several years, including in his own firm Blockrandbebauung – Architektur + Philosophie from 2007 to 2014. During this time, he mainly worked in the areas of building in existing fabric and monument protection. In addition, he dedicated himself to academic work as a philosopher. From 2012 to 2016, Düchs was an associate member of the Professional Code Committee of the Bavarian Chamber of Architects (Bayerische Architektenkammer). In 2018, he was appointed an extraordinary member of the Association of German Architects (BDA). In 2011, Düchs was awarded the title Dr. phil. for a doctoral thesis on the ethics of the architect. Since 2014, he has been working as a research associate at the Chair of Philosophy II at the University of Bamberg. He was a Visiting Fellow at Clare Hall College, Cambridge, UK in 2017 and completed his habilitation on the question of human images in architecture two years later.

1 Theodor W. Adorno, *Minima moralia: Reflexionen aus dem beschädigten Leben*, Frankfurt a. M. 2001 [1st ed. 1951], pp. 40ff.

2 This publication and the website www. dbxchange.eu (accessed 30 November 2019), documenting an increasing number and variety of DesignBuild projects, can serve as evidence.

3 I understand "ethics" (synonym: moral philosophy) to be a science in which moral statements, ideas, and ideals and their normative and eudemonistic implications are discussed, criticized and/or justified rationally and intersubjectively in a comprehensible manner. In turn, I consider "moral" to imply the customs, standards, and traditions that are relevant in a society, without their explicit and rational justification. Ethics (or moral philosophy) are therefore based on morals, while morals are conceivable without ethics. In this regard cf. Wilhelm Vossenkuhl, *Die Möglichkeit des Guten*, Munich 2006; Martin Düchs, *Architektur für ein gutes Leben: Über Verantwortung, Moral und Ethik des Architekten*, Münster 2011; regarding the question of the scientific nature of ethics Julian Nida-Rümelin, "Theoretische und angewandte Ethik: Paradigmen, Begründungen, Bereiche," in: Julian Nida-Rümelin (ed.), *Angewandte Ethik: Die Bereichsethiken und ihre theoretische Fundierung*, 2nd ed., Stuttgart 2005, pp. 2–87.

4 I use the term "constructions" broadly here to describe the creative modification of a pre-existing situation. Playgrounds or gardens can therefore also be described as constructions in this sense. Regarding the underlying architectural term, please refer to Martin Düchs, "Architektur muss brennen, aber darf Architekturwissenschaft brennen? Zur Frage der Legitimität normativer Aussagen in der Architekturwissenschaft," in: Karsten Berr and Achim Hahn (eds.), *Interdisziplinäre Architektur-Wissenschaft [working title])*, Wiesbaden 2019/2020 (forthcoming).

5 The mentioned focus on doing and/or concrete experience can also be understood as a response to an overemphasis on the theoretical approach to architecture in the 1960s and 1970s. Consider for example the intellectually highly complex writings and constructions

by Peter Eisenman (Peter Eisenman, *Aura und Exzeß: Zur Überwindung der Metaphysik der Architektur*, Vienna 1995; Peter Eisenman, *Ins Leere geschrieben: [1995–2000]*, Vienna 2005), which architects like Jacques Herzog and Pierre de Meuron find baffling, because they claim to want to make sensory experiences possible rather than ideas: "The strength of our buildings is the immediate visceral response they have on a visitor. For us, that is all that is important in architecture. We want to make a building that can cause sensations, not represent this or that idea." (Richard C. Levene et al. (eds.), *Herzog & De Meuron 1981–2000 (El Croquis 60+84)*, Madrid 2005, p. 35). For Eisenman, on the other hand (at least in the 1970s and 1980s), precisely the intellectual ideas are of importance to architecture. This specific contradiction is also very evident in a discussion between Christopher Alexander and Peter Eisenman (Peter Eisenman and Christopher Alexander, "Harmonie und Ganzheitlichkeit in der Architektur – Ein Streitgespräch" [1983], in: Ulrich Schwarz (ed.), *Aura und Exzeß: Zur Überwindung der Metaphysik der Architektur*, Vienna 1995, p. 229). In this regard cf. Kenneth Frampton, *Studies in Tectonic Culture: The Poetics of Construction in Nineteenth and Twentieth Century Architecture*, Cambridge, MA 1995; Otl Aicher, "architektur und erkenntnistheorie," in: Otl Aicher (ed.), *analog und digital*, Berlin 1991, pp. 92–107; Harry Francis Mallgrave, *Modern Architectural Theory: A Historical Survey, 1673–1968*. Cambridge 2009; Harry Francis Mallgrave and David Goodman, *An Introduction to Architectural Theory: 1968 to the Present*, Malden, MA. 2011.

6 The projects named in this publication can serve as examples.

7 Cf. Douglas Spencer, *The Architecture of Neoliberalism: How Contemporary Architecture Became an Instrument of Control and Compliance*, London 2016.

8 Massimiliano Fuksas and Doriana O. Mandrelli (eds.), *Città: Less Aesthetics, More Ethics*, Venice 2000. The exhibition Small Scale, Big Change at the Museum of Modern Art in New York, curated by Andres Lepik in 2010, also contributed to reinforcing the trend

towards social building. Cf. Andres Lepik, *Small Scale, Big Change: New Architectures of Social Engagement*, exhibition catalogue, Museum of Modern Art, New York 2010.

9 For more information, cf. Martin Düchs, *Architektur für ein gutes Leben: Über Verantwortung, Moral und Ethik des Architekten*, Münster 2011; Martin Düchs, "Von der Verantwortung zur Ethik des Architekten – und zurück: Ein Vorschlag in vier Leistungsphasen gem. HOAI," in: Achim Hahn (ed.), *Ausdruck und Gebrauch. Dresdner wissenschaftliche Halbjahreshefte für Architektur – Wohnen – Umwelt/ Ausdruck und Gebrauch: Themenheft: Positionen einer Architektur- und Planungsethik*, Herzogenrath 2014; Martin Düchs, *50+1 Architektonische Gewissensfragen: answered by Dr. Martin Düchs with a foreword by Dr. Dr. Rainer Erlinger*, Munich 2019.

10 In this regard and for all other quotes by Adorno, unless otherwise stated, cf. Theodor W. Adorno, "Funktionalismus heute" [1965], in: *Kulturkritik und Gesellschaft I (Gesammelte Schriften 10.1)*, Darmstadt 1997, pp. 375–395.

11 Ibid.

12 Ibid.

13 Adorno uses the expression "transcendentally homeless" in a letter to Leo Löwenthal, which he composed together with Siegfried Kracauer. They state the sender of the letter as the Welfare Bureau for the Transcendentally Homeless. Cf. in this regard and quoting Martin Mittermeier, "Es gibt kein richtiges Sich-Ausstrecken in der falschen Badewanne: Wie Adornos berühmtester Satz wirklich lautet – ein Gang ins Archiv" ("You can't stretch out properly in the wrong bathtub: What Adorno's most famous sentence really is – a visit to the archives"), in: *Recherche. Zeitung für Wissenschaft* 3/4 2009.

14 Martin Heidegger, "Bauen Wohnen Denken," in: Otto Bartning (ed.), *Mensch und Raum: 2. Darmstädter Gespräch 1951*, Darmstadt 1952, p. 84.

15 Karsten Harries has spelled out Heidegger's considerations regarding existential homelessness and described fighting it as an "ethical function of architecture." Cf. Karsten Harries, *The Ethical Function of Architecture,* London 1997. Cf. as comment on this: Martin Düchs and Christian Illies, "Wer wohnt hier eigentlich? Eine unzeitgemäße anthropologische Fussnote zu The Ethical Function of Architecture," *Wolkenkuckucksheim* 22 (36), 2017, pp. 87–113.

16 In this regard, cf. https://homenotshelter. com (accessed 30 November 2019).

17 Cf. Otl Aicher, "architektur und erkenntnistheorie," in: Otl Aicher (ed.) *analog und digital*, Berlin 1991, p. 106.

18 Many descriptions of the approach are encouraging, however, since at least in many instances there seems to be an awareness of the importance of a theoretical foundation. For an example in this regard, cf. https://www.code. tu-berlin.de/design-build.php (accessed 30 November 2019).

Learning by Doing

In a DesignBuild studio, students experience the complexity and broad scope of the processes involved in an architectural project by completing them personally, starting from the first idea and sketch and culminating in actually realizing the construction. Students work collaboratively, forming a large team, and bear the responsibilities and consequences of their actions collectively. They learn how to cope with small budgets, tight schedules and unexpected problems, and – most importantly – are confronted with the friction that generally occurs when plans are turned into built reality.

As an action-oriented teaching method, DesignBuild represents an ideal situation for acquiring relevant practical skills and abilities, which includes interdisciplinary qualifications such as social competence and self-competence. "Learning by doing" plays a major role in this context. The focus is on a reciprocal learning process that takes place between the different parties involved in the project. In our studio, this is also reinforced by the fact that, in the design phase, solution proposals are not evolved by the students in competition with each other but instead by joint discussion of concepts and collective development.

Another significant aspect of DesignBuild projects is that all planning and building work is carried out by the same participants, without the strict separation between design and building that is common in customary architectural practice. This gives students an opportunity to develop the design along with the building process. The hands-on building process can open up potential ideas and experiences that, in turn, can lead to a change or regeneration of the design.

The aim of our DesignBuild projects is however not reduced to the realization of a construction, but is more about giving students an opportunity to experience and understand the immediate effects of their thinking, communication, and actions in a broader context.

Peter Fattinger is head of design. build studio, which he founded at TU Vienna in 2000. His dissertation "Design-Build-Studio. Rahmenbedingungen, Prozesse und Potentiale von Design-Build-Projekten in der Architekturausbildung" ("Design-Build-Studio. Framework Conditions, Processes and Potentials of Design-Build Projects in Architectural Education") investigated DesignBuild as an action-oriented teaching method. He is co-founder of the European DesignBuild Knowledge Network and the network Design for the Common Good. Together with Veronika Orso, he runs the design and fabrication studio fattinger orso. architektur, which operates at the intersection of architecture, art, and design.

add on. 20 höhenmeter, temporary installation by Peter Fattinger, Veronika Orso, Michael Rieper and students of the design.build studio of the TU Vienna, Vienna Brigittenau 2005

| HILDE STROBL

"Architecture Has Become Too Important to Be Left to Architects."

PARTICIPATIVE PLANNING AND BUILDING STRATEGIES

HILDE STROBL

"Planning together and not only designing a building, but also constructing it – that gave me a completely different view of my job as an architect," sums up a student of the Munich University of Applied Sciences after a DesignBuild project in Quiané, Mexico. For many architects, simply the idea of sharing the authoritative decision-making power regarding the design and working together with laypersons is already a nightmare. It is necessary, however, to distinguish between planning processes that involve the users, and planning strategies that furthermore rely on a collective authorship of the designers – as is common in DesignBuild projects.

Participation as a challenge to the architect's self-image
Although many universities and universities of applied sciences offer DesignBuild studios, they are hardly able to meet the huge demand. Dietmar Steiner thinks that one reason for the success of the Design-Build movement may be that academic teaching has increasingly moved away from building practice in the last decades. This could in turn be caused by the fact that the components of building are becoming ever more complex: "The key difference between artificial building experiments at universities and projects on location in socially precarious situations is the contact to reality, or: the direct confrontation of architecture with life. This aspect teaches female students in particular that there is a real need for their knowledge and skills, that they can solve problems with their ideas and actions, rather than – like in academic experiments – merely creating them."[1] Yet there continues to be a discrepancy between the enthusiasm of the participants and a lacking acceptance by architects in general.
The question of what value can be attributed to the experience gained in DesignBuild studios for further work as an architect is particularly contended. The fact that there is an increasing demand for using participative methods, as practiced – to a greater or lesser extent – in the studios, is illustrated by the ubiquitous development of democratic

◄
**DesignBuild Studio
Quiané in Santa
Catarina, Mexico**

social movements calling for participation in the design of urban spaces and large projects. In addition, an increasing number of cooperatives are currently being founded, whose planning processes are also based on principles of participation, but which lack architects who know how to deal with participative processes.

Quoting Susanne Hofmann of Die Baupiloten BDA (originally in German): If the quality of architecture is measured by "its sustainable usability and the degree of identification of the user with the building [...] great importance must be attached to their participation in the shaping of their environment. [...] The often implicit knowledge of people about spatial qualities and their requirements regarding the utilization and experience of spaces is a social potential that architecture must take into account. [...] Participation is therefore also a challenge to the self-image of architects, since a participative design and building process may also generate new production methods and new building aesthetics."[2]

Participation as an antithesis to authoritarian architecture

In the late 1970s, Hermann Czech warned against architects giving up power, insisting that architecture was giving up its ambition when people and "those who listen only to what the people say" gained control of form-finding processes.[3] With this, Czech positioned himself against the many voices in the 1960s demanding a change from radical large-scale measures and top-down planning to taking on social responsibility. Jane Jacobs's *The Death and Life of Great American Cities* (1961) caused a debate on the influence of architecture on society.[4] The focus was no longer only on the form, but also on the social contexts of creation and society-related issues, and these played a role in collective bottom-up processes. Architects such as Walter Segal and Yona Friedman developed participative self-construction concepts,[5] while Giancarlo De Carlo formulated a theoretical manifesto for participation in architecture. In *Architecture's Public* (1970), De Carlo argued that participation could be a proof of planning quality and simultaneously an opportunity to overcome the legitimation crisis of architecture. He ascribed this to the contradiction that architecture was closer to the interests of money and power than to the everyday life of the users of the building.[6] Hence De Carlo distinguished between planning "for" and "with" users, and introduced variables that allowed a permanent verification of use and feasibility, preventing consolidation of a once-reached consensus and permitting its adaptation at any time in the course of planning.

Drawing workshop for the Tacloban project in Leyte, Philippines

| HILDE STROBL

"But in reality, participation needs to transform architectural planning from the authoritarian act, which it has been up to now, into a process. This process begins with the discovery of the users' needs, passing through the formulation of formal and organizational hypotheses before entering the phase of use. Here, instead of reaching its usual full stop, the process must be reopened in a continuous alternation of controls and reformulations [...]."[7] To treat users as "representatives of new values" and to also bear the "subversive consequences," meant for De Carlo to radically question "all the traditional value systems which, since they were built on non-participation, must be revised or replaced."[8] De Carlo's provocative thesis, that "architecture has become too important to be left to architects" called for a structural change.[9] He demanded a process-oriented understanding of planning, based on feedback between users and designers. This means that the architect abandons the traditional role as a creator to become an agitator for architecture instead.

Participation and DesignBuild

The actors involved in the participative processes of DesignBuild projects include students and lecturers as well as users. The extent to which practical realization corresponds to participation theory depends both on the particular participants and project-related factors – and also on a willingness to bear the consequences of participation.

Dialogic learning

At the beginning of a DesignBuild project, the analysis of the context and the building site is focused on querying, gathering and evaluating data on the local situation, usage requirements, and user wishes, but dialogic learning is also required. A feedback process involving users and partner organizations on site makes it possible to explore local conditions, building methods, building materials and traditions, to make feasibility studies, and from this, to develop a design concept and building construction.

Collective planning

The time span and physical distance between the planning phase at the universities and universities of applied sciences and actual commencement of building on site necessitate focused planning processes in which the group of students works collectively and yet at the same time allocates specific tasks. To this end, different skills are brought together and sub-responsibilities are assumed by individual group members. An important factor for the planning process is to make sure that

Presentation of Maison pour tous project to the Municipality of Four

Interim assessment of Maison pour tous project at École Nationale Supérieure d'Architecture de Grenoble

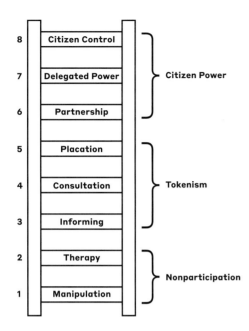

8	Citizen Control	}	Citizen Power
7	Delegated Power		
6	Partnership		
5	Placation	}	Tokenism
4	Consultation		
3	Informing		
2	Therapy	}	Nonparticipation
1	Manipulation		

individual, less assertive participants are not excluded through the dynamics of the group, resulting in an originally inclusive approach becoming exclusive. Students and lecturers benefit equally from a diversity of ideas. Intensive discussion is essential to creating confidence in the feasibility of the project and hence forms a prerequisite for the power of a team.

Participation as hypothesis

The degree of participation of the locals in the building process varies for different projects. Ideally, building work would take place "at eye level," with a mutual exchange of knowledge and methods used. The sociopolitical dimension of learning from each other plays a special role in this regard. The process as such does not, however, end with this. Acceptance and functionality will only become apparent when the building is actually used. This is the responsibility of the steering organization on the one hand, while user behavior and the extent of identification are reflected by the degree of participation during the entire process on the other. The Ladder of Citizen Participation is a model developed by Sherry Arnstein in the late 1960s that describes the different levels of participation of citizens in planning and hence the degrees of power not only to be involved in decisions, but to make them.[10] The hypothetical model refers to the relationship of urban society and urban politics, but has also been adopted again and again in DesignBuild, particularly with regard to planning processes. Arnstein starts at the lowest rung of the ladder with the lowest degree of involvement of participants. The consequence is manipulation – the users merely taking over measures conceived by others. A "partnership" – as desired between local representatives and universities in the realization of DesignBuild projects – is depicted in the upper third, and can be considered equivalent to project development "at eye level". At the top of the ladder of participation is citizen control, where users have absolute control of all processes. In the case of DesignBuild projects, this would require for all participants that no distinction is made between support and aid on the one hand and planners and construction management on the other. Therefore, indirect participation cannot be presumed in participatory processes – instead, participation means direct influence.

Architectural practice in progress

If one assumes that students are confronted with participative methods in DesignBuild studios and that these become a fixed component in architectural training, then this would be a step towards a change in architectural practice in the long term. Extensive participatory processes are not however always present on both the user and planner level and within the collective planning procedure. The personal experiences of students as well as their assessment of the impact on their academic studies were for instance evaluated by the Thinking While Doing network[12] for the field of DesignBuild education. A large number of students were satisfied with the built result and their own performance, they enjoyed working hard, and felt good in the group. The survey showed that students considered the frequency of group discussions to be acceptable and their experience meaningfully applicable to architectural practice – there were, however, no concrete questions regarding the participatory process between the actors. But which are the most important factors that would help to reduce the barriers of participation in DesignBuild? Different examples show that

Sherry Arnstein's "Ladder of Citizen Participation," 1969

participatory processes increase with the reduction of barriers in the language and culture of students and users. Projects in the vicinity of schools of architecture enable a more intensive exchange. This is demonstrated by early examples such as a student housing project from the 1980s in Stuttgart-Vaihingen (Peter Sulzer, Peter Hübner et al.)[12] or projects by Rural Studio in Alabama, and the interaction "addon. 20 höhenmeter" in Vienna Brigittenau by Peter Fattinger and Veronika Orso,[13] or the urban interventions of Jesko Fezer.[14] For the purpose of participation – and hence the extension of architectural practice – this would suggest an increased focus on the immediate spheres of influence of universities and universities of applied sciences. To quote Peter Blundell Jones in *Architecture and Participation*: participation "is not just a catalyst for transformation of the role (and eventual lives) of users, but also for the transformation of architectural practice."[15]

Hilde Strobl is an architectural historian and curator. She studied art history and German language and literature and completed her studies with a doctoral thesis on the work of Wolfgang Hildesheimer. From 2005 to 2019, she worked at the Architecture Museum and the Chair of Architectural History and Curatorial Studies at the Technical University of Munich (TUM). As a curator, she focuses on the social relevance of architecture in her exhibitions and publications, as well as in her media work such as "Show & Tell. Architekturgeschichte(n) aus der Sammlung" (2014), "ZOOM! Architektur und Stadt im Bild" (2015), "Keine Angst vor Partizipation! – Wohnen heute" (2016), "Wohnungen, Wohnungen, Wohnungen! Die Geschichte des Wohnungsbaus in Bayern 1918|2018" (2018), and "Die Neue Heimat (1950–1982). Eine sozialdemokratische Utopie und ihre Bauten" (2019). In July 2019, Hilde Strobl was commissioned by the Austrian State of Tyrol to conduct on-going research on architecture of the Nazi era.

1 Dietmar Steiner, "Die Design-Build-Bewegung," in: *Arch+*, 211/212, 2013, pp. 152f., here p. 153.

2 Susanne Hofmann, *Partizipation macht Architektur. Die Baupiloten – Methode und Projekte*, Berlin 2014, pp. 8f.

3 Hermann Czech, "Manierismus und Partizipation" [1977], in: Gerd de Bruyn, Stephan Trüby (ed.), *architektur_theorie.doc. texte seit 1960*, Basel 2003, pp. 243–245, here p. 243.

4 Jane Jacobs, *The Death and Life of Great American Cities*, New York 1961 (German edition: *Tod und Leben großer amerikanischer Städte*, Berlin 1963; on the architect as a "social engineer" cf. Sonja Hnilica, *Der Glaube an das Große in der Architektur der Moderne. Großstrukturen der 1960er und 1970er Jahre*, Zurich 2018, pp. 170–174. Also cf. Heike Delitz, *Gebaute Gesellschaft. Architektur als Medium des Sozialen*, Frankfurt a.M. 2010.

5 See Peter Blundell Jones, "Sixty-Eight and After," in: Peter Blundell Jones, Doina Petrescu, Jeremy Till (ed.), *Architecture and Participation*, New York 2005, pp. 132–148; John McKean, *Learning from Segal. Von Segal lernen*, Basel/Boston/Berlin 1989; Yona Friedman, *Meine Fibel. Wie die Stadtbewohner ihre Häuser und Städte selber planen können*, Düsseldorf 1974.

6 Giancarlo De Carlo, "Architecture's Public. The Revolt and the Frustration of the School of Architecture," in: *Arch+*, 211/212, 2013, pp. 87–95, here p. 92.

7 Ibid., p. 94.

8 Ibid.

9 Ibid., p. 92.

10 Sherry R. Arnstein, "A Ladder of Citizen Participation," in: *Journal of the American Institute of Planners*, 35 (4), 1969, pp. 216–224.

11 Stephen Verderber, Ted Cavanagh, Arlene Oak (eds.), *Thinking While Doing. Explorations in Educational Design/Build*, Basel 2019, pp. 199f.

12 Peter Sulzer et al. (eds.), *Lernen durch Selberbauen. Ein Beitrag zur praxisorientierten Architektenausbildung*, Karlsruhe 1983.

13 Peter Fattinger, Veronika Orso, Michael Rieper (eds.), *addon. 20 höhenmeter*, Vienna/Bolzano 2008.

14 Jesko Fezer, Matthias Heyden (eds.), *MetroZones 3. Hier entsteht. Strategien partizipativer Architektur und räumlicher Aneignung*, Berlin 2004.

15 Peter Blundell Jones, Doina Petrescu, Jeremy Till (eds.), *Architecture and Participation*, New York 2005, pp. XII–XV, here p. XIV (transl. by author)

| BERNADETTE HEIERMANN AND JUDITH REITZ

About DesignBuild

Bernadette Heiermann and Judith Reitz

As elements of architectural studies, DesignBuild projects raise research-relevant questions for us as lecturers, as well as for students, which go far beyond mere building. Innovative and holistic ideas regarding material, construction, program, process, participation, community, and sustainability are in the foreground.

We ask:

Where and in which culture are we researching and building?

Who will inhabit/use our project?

Who are our partners, who are the long-term users?

What added value is created for the community?

How can we use traditional materials for modern building and for exploring new directions?

What potential do recycled materials have as building materials?

How can we develop authentic buildings whose aesthetics respond to place and culture?

How will users and neighbors react to the aesthetics of the design?

How can we realize our plans on site together with users, vocational schools and craftspeople and how can they additionally function as multipliers?

What partners of which interdisciplinary subject areas do we want to collaborate with for projects?

What remains after we leave?

We learn:

Collaboration on an equal footing with an academic partner on site, in direct contact with local communities, is an essential prerequisite for a sustainable DesignBuild project in a global context. This includes a balanced transfer of knowledge in both directions as well as facilitation of equal mobility; in an ideal case, DesignBuild projects would be developed at a European university with partners from the Global South. A "post-occupancy evaluation" should be an integral part of the process in the sense of a holistic approach.

The experience gained by students within the context of DesignBuild projects on topics such as relevance of the future profession and responsibility, handling of material, and craftsmanship as well as (global) exchange is incomparable.

DesignBuild programs should therefore become a fixed component of the curricula of architectural faculties!

Bernadette Heiermann is an architect who, along with running her architectural practice Heiermann Architekten, teaches at the Chair of Building Typologies and Design Basics at the RWTH Aachen. She is interested in a holistic approach combining conceptual design, planning, and technical realization in the context of full-scale projects.

Judith Reitz teaches at PBSA/University of Applied Sciences Düsseldorf, with a focus on fundamentals of design and conceptual interior design as well as realization of experimental full-scale projects. Next to her architectural office bfr-lab Architekten, she is a lecturer at RWTH Aachen.

Together, Heiermann and Reitz created the Design.Develop.Build program. Their work in Southern Africa has been awarded numerous prizes.

◄
Interior of Guga S'Thebe Theater, Cape Town, South Africa

►►
Performance at the Guga S'Thebe Theater, Cape Town, South Africa

| BERNADETTE HEIERMANN AND JUDITH REITZ

On Building in a Different Culture

**Interview with architects Lorena Burbano and Sebastián Oviedo, from *Atarraya Taller de Arquitectura* in Quito, Ecuador.
The interview for TUM Architecture Museum was conducted by Vera Simone Bader.**

In 2017, the German newspaper *Die Zeit* dedicated a long article to high school graduates and college students who volunteer as social workers in underdeveloped places, and accused them of doing so mainly to clear their conscience. How do you see these arguments in relation to the DesignBuild projects being implemented by white students in Latin America or Africa? They, too, are often accused of making a neocolonial gesture. Where, do you think, is the problem?

We find it hard to make an overarching statement for all of Design-Build. Nevertheless, we think the greatest potential for conflict lies in that most of these projects, in their involvement with historically marginalized communities, engage with, and benefit from colonial asymmetries.

Each program, project, and individual deals with this differently. They can position themselves anywhere within a spectrum that ranges from actively working to dismantle those asymmetries, to deliberately taking advantage of

them, or to naively ignoring them. But most of them operate within a shared context where they are on the privileged end of an asymmetry. By this, we mean the historical construction of unequal ways of assigning and distributing opportunity, value, and power. This is not exclusive to situations where Europeans or North Americans go to Latin America or Africa – it is present even when working in one's own country or city.

The article you refer to criticizes the questionable results of programs where volunteers are completely unqualified for their work. The subtext suggests that their qualification is, in fact, in being European – their origin entitles them to do this work, without much evaluation. Similarly, many Design-Build projects can only be carried out thanks to the privilege that allows formally educated students to build in marginalized communities, without much scrutiny. This is even more true for North-South programs and, although it does not automatically mean that they should not be carried out, we think we should acknowledge that the circumstances allowing this have colonial roots.

Even though these projects are usually not run by for-profit agencies, they involve other types of value extraction. The academic institutions, teaching staff, and students behind these projects use them for their own economic, cultural, and symbolic advantage. Whether this is fair or not, largely

depends on what they contribute in exchange. In many cases, Design-Build projects have a material outcome of high quality. They not only bring their well-meaning presence to these places, but in fact make funding, labour, and knowledge available to communities that would otherwise have no access to them. But there are also cases that experiment and take unnecessary risks, build structures of dubious durability or structural integrity, show up to a construction site without any drawings or execution planning, initiate projects that have not been requested by communities, and so on. Rather than making themselves and their skills available to these communities, one could argue that they use historically marginalized peoples and places as a testing lab or a marketing platform.

Although the material outcome is maybe the most visible component of DesignBuild projects, we should resist evaluating them solely based on their performance as providers of buildings. Even if the built object

Traditional dance groups performing at the inauguration of the Center for Culture and Ecology in Santa Catarina Quiané, Mexico

The Chamanga Cultural Center is the result of a two-year collaboration between local organization Opción Más, Atarraya Taller de Arquitectura, Munich University of Applied Sciences, Portland State University, and University of Tokyo

▶
Workshop for the Chamanga Cultural Centre, Ecuador

Interim meeting with Opción Más, students and local artists for the Chamanga Cultural Centre, Ecuador

is of high quality, the approach or process can be questionable. Using a by-default privileged position to push own values and priorities, promoting projects that have not been requested by communities, framing structural inequalities as design opportunities or exaggerating the role of outsiders and buildings while minimizing local collective struggles in tackling injustices, are some of the harmful dynamics that come to our mind. The narratives built around these projects can also be conflictive. An example of this is when marginalized regions and peoples are described as if they were aesthetic experiences or touristic destinations to be enjoyed or "saved". In a sort of spectacle of the non-European, the "exotic" nature of the other is exploited to attract potential donors, employers, or new students, as mentioned in the article by *Die Zeit*. This is something to be particularly wary of as DesignBuild becomes increasingly popular and therefore marketable.

How could things be different?

We believe that, in addition to structuring, approaching, and developing these projects with good intentions, we should deepen the discussion of the broader structural conditions under which we operate. These projects are not happening in an ahistorical, apolitical, post-racial vacuum. Nothing is. And we need to be aware of this to eliminate the risk of ignoring, and therefore perpetuating,

colonial dynamics. For us, the best option would be to approach this work with a deliberately decolonial agenda to be observed at every stage and level of decision-making. This goes all the way from the organization of projects (which types of initiatives we support, with whom, how, and why) to the more personal level. Asymmetrical distributions of power, opportunity, and value can only be defied and eroded when we are able to identify and interpret them in their complex historical context. Developing this type of awareness takes more than a one-semester studio, and designing and building a structure is already incredibly challenging on its own. But we choose to engage with these complexities, and therefore it is our responsibility to do so in the most conscious and intentional way we can.

Is it even possible to implement DesignBuild projects abroad without asymmetries?

Well, these asymmetries do not exist exclusively within DesignBuild projects, but are rather structural. This means that they need to be tackled as such: eliminating them is a task that will take time and effort from different sectors of society. So unfortunately, our answer would be: not yet. DesignBuild projects, whether abroad or not, always operate within these asymmetries. If the structural inequalities remain ignored, we will, despite our good intentions, default to

dynamics and narratives that reproduce and legitimize them. However, if we acknowledge them, we can challenge them. We would like to think that Design-Build, in its collaboration with community organizations and social movements, has the potential to help tackle some of these structural issues. Not only because of its material outcomes, but also because of the opportunities it creates to defy and modify imaginaries and assumptions in those directly involved, as well as in broader society.

Do you find this experience important? Or should DesignBuild rather take place exclusively in one's own country?

The pedagogical value of Design-Build is, we think, well known and demonstrated. From a technical and constructive standpoint it is very valuable, as it allows participants to experience the process of design, planning, and construction as a whole. This, in turn, creates opportunities to better understand the relationships and interdependencies throughout these processes. Many programs also integrate pre-design, fundraising, or documentation, which broadens the scope of these projects and the type of knowledge and skills that participants develop. DesignBuild projects also create immense learning opportunities in terms of "soft skills": teamwork, cultural competence, communication, among others. They allow

participants to develop an understanding of and appreciation for the labor and skills of peers such as carpenters, masons, metalworkers and other construction tradespeople, engineers, architects, landscape architects, and others involved. These are very valuable experiences.

Projects abroad perhaps add some complexity to the learning opportunities, as they increase the participants' level of exposure to different ways of knowing and living. This means that they can develop a deeper understanding of themselves and others. At the same time, we think the experience is both important and potentially conflictive regardless of whether participants go abroad or not. We have participated in Design-Build projects in our home country, Ecuador, with students from Ecuador and other Latin American countries, in the USA with students from the USA, and in Mexico and Ecuador with students from Europe, the USA, locals, and other fellow Latin Americans. All of these were valuable experiences for everyone involved.

Nevertheless, what we think is at stake in the discussion of Design-Build projects is not whether they are valuable for the students and academic institutions behind them. The question is whether these projects are in the best interest of the communities they engage with. Whether they are an adequate contribution to the collective processes led by these communi-

ties, one that represents their own values, priorities, and agendas. Whether the academic participants of projects are aware of their biases and privileges, and work to prevent them from driving decision-making. It is simultaneously a political and a technical question, so discussion and incorporation of knowledge and theory from other fields, particularly the social sciences, is crucial.

What is your advice for students traveling to other countries to implement a DesignBuild project? What should they pay attention to? What about instructors?
We think the most important thing to pay attention to is the way a project is structured – what kind of project it is, with whom, where, and so on. We advocate seeing these projects as opportunities to accompany and support local autonomous processes. This means that we should only go to where we have been invited to contribute, making sure that we are making ourselves available to the specific demands and requests of these communities, rather than finding places that meet what we want to research or build.

Then, we think we absolutely have to make sure that the architectural and construction work is done responsibly and respectfully, that it does not take risks, is durable and well planned, structurally sound, climatically adequate, culturally appropriate, and so on. In terms of decision-making, we need to make

sure that we are only making the decisions that we were explicitly asked to make, providing information and creating opportunities for users and the broader community to lead and guide our work throughout the process.

In general, we think we need to be careful of doing things that reinforce a sense of superiority, or that reproduce attitudes and narratives of the saviors and the saved. We suggest to pay attention to understanding ourselves and the buildings we help produce as secondary to the collective efforts of the communities we work with, who must be the ones making the decisions. Our collaborators, both individually and collectively, must be recognized as active subjects with their own trajectories and agendas, rather than as beneficiaries or contexts of intervention.

At the same time, accusations of DesignBuild being colonial demand that we acknowledge a deeper level of conflict. Other disciplines such as anthropology or pedagogy, in their efforts to eliminate their colonial roles and biases, have engaged in constant evaluation, discussion, and modification of their epistemological and methodological basis, their underlying assumptions and expected out-

Opción Más leaders during a discussion on dry toilets and design options of the Chamanga Cultural Center

Lunchtime at the Chamanga Cultural Center – women from Opción Más prepare meals for children

comes, their history, use, and position as disciplines in context. Over several decades, they have assumed this as a permanent and long-lasting challenge. We think that the same should apply to architecture. As the profession expects to operate in sectors of society that it has traditionally excluded, it needs to think about its underlying assumptions, its historic biases, and to fundamentally modify itself. We engage with a reality that is very different from the classic client-architect relationship that the profession and education are based upon, and we cannot expect to do so with the same knowledge, skills, or attitude.

If we really want DesignBuild to be free of any accusation of being colonial, we need to look at the discipline and education as a whole. DesignBuild and other applied projects can play a very significant role in modifying the profession and education, but we cannot limit the discussion to these projects, much less to the five or eight weeks spent on-site.

Is the responsibility that the students assume for the project sufficient?

In our experience, students usually approach these projects with a very high level of responsibility, dedication, and determination. This translates to very hard, thoughtful work in planning, fundraising, and on the construction site. The projects usually require immense amounts of effort and energy, and students get very engaged because they find it motivating and noticeably more meaningful than design studios which only have a print outcome.

At the same time, students usually operate within a set framework – the project has already been defined and, with it, the partners, location, and motivations, the approach and theoretical perspective have been set, the studio calendar, and sometimes even the program as well. In this sense, we need to make sure that the students' hard work and sense

of responsibility is going towards solving a problem that was correctly defined and represents the values and priorities of the community, within a framework that allows all of us to think of these projects as more complex than just spatial or constructive challenges. In most cases, instructors are the ones who make the most critical decisions, as they set the logistical, technical, and theoretical framework within which students operate.

Some programs engage students in pre-design as well, or are completely student-run, which allows them to take part in problem-definition stages, go through processes of community participation and engagement, project identification and development, and so on. This is an advantage of being on-site: the project can be more easily framed and structured as a long-term collaboration process rather than as a product to be built or delivered.

How can one better integrate the local universities and achieve a balanced relationship?

Working with strong local groups who connect the rather episodic presence of DesignBuild projects with longer-term processes of community engagement is indeed very important. And local universities are certainly a very good option – they have their particular trajectories and therefore provide different, enriching perspectives, have important contextual knowledge, and so on. We think collaboration between academic institutions should be pursued whenever possible, as both sides can benefit. In Latin America, in particular, several universities and programs have a long-lasting tradition of respectful, responsible, and transparent support of social, popular, and indigenous organizations and movements in their countries, from which we think there is much to learn. The same can be said of other kinds of local organizations in the region that are not exclusively academic.

Nevertheless, we should be careful of thinking that colonial dynamics, attitudes, and asymmetries are only a result of the national origin of participants. Universities and organizations who support the work of social movements or community organizations and collaborate with them in a respectful, responsible, and committed way are not good at it because of which country they come from, but because of how they discuss the context of their work, how they see their role in this context, and how they carry it out. And we think this is what we should all strive to do, regardless of where we work or where we come from.

Lorena Burbano and Sebastián Oviedo are architects from Quito, Ecuador. In 2016, they started Atarraya Taller de Arquitectura, an architecture studio that collaborates with community organizations and grassroots processes of environmental action.

Their collaboration with the inhabitants of Chamanga, a town of fisher people severely affected by the 2016 earthquake in Ecuador, led them to co-organize and teach at several programs with civil society organizations, public entities, and academic institutions from Ecuador, Germany, Japan, Spain, Australia, and the USA. The processes and results of their collaborative work in Chamanga, including the planning and construction of the Cultural Center with the local cultural collective Opción Más and in cooperation with Munich Unversity of Applied Sciences (MUAS), Portland State University, and University of Tokyo, have been recognized with serveral international awards.

Since 2018, they have co-taught the DesignBuild studio at Prof. Ursula Hartig's Chair for Planning and Building in a Global Context at MUAS, supporting a community center for culture and ecology in rural Oaxaca, Mexico.

The Chamanga Cultural
Center is not only used
by teenagers as planned,
but also by children

ON BUILDING IN A DIFFERENT CULTURE

Experiences

Interview with students Helena Brückner, Shpresa Cekaj, Moritz Klein, Martin Mitterhofer, and Franziska Odametey, at the Department of Architecture at the Technical University of Munich (TUM), Chair of Architectural Design and Timber Construction.
The interview for the Architecture Museum of TUM was conducted by Vera Simone Bader.

◄
Preparing the circular footing for the school building in Pepel in Sierra Leone, TUM, 2018/2019

▲
Surveying the site for the school building

You all participated in the DesignBuild project involving construction of a school in Pepel/Sierra Leone, offered by TUM to students taking the Master degree course in Architectural Design and Timber Construction in 2018/2019. Had you ever been to Africa before?
Moritz Klein: No, I had never been to Africa.
Martin Mitterhofer: I had never been there either.
Shpresa Cekaj: Me neither.
Helena Brückner: I come from Namibia.
Franziska Odametey: I had been to Ghana. I participated in a different project there. I really wanted to do this because my father comes from Ghana and I'd never been there.

How long did you stay in Sierra Leone?
Martin Mitterhofer: We spent a total of two and a half months there.

Where did you stay?
Martin Mitterhofer: We stayed in Pepel itself, in the center of the village, at a former entertainment complex that was built by the British at the time. It is now used for events in the village. The building was converted into a dormitory for us.
Helena Brückner: It was the only building of that size in the whole village, and the villagers let us use it. That's when we started to realise what an effort they made for us, also financially. They really looked after us very well.

Could you get in touch with the people directly through your accommodation?
Franziska Odametey: Unfortunately, we did not get in touch with the villagers through the accommodation, as the building was enclosed by a wall and so the villagers couldn't get inside. That was a shame, because it made meeting spontaneously away from the construction site nearly impossible. There were people who cooked for us and even something like a security service, which we found strange and a bit awkward at first. But with time, we got closer to them as they were always around. We got to know each other better, which was nice.

Martin Mitterhofer: But everyone knew that we were there. The building was also located right in front of a football field, so there was always something going on. The children of the village waited in front of the building and walked with us to the building site and back. In the end, it felt like we were part of the village.

So what did you do all day?
Martin Mitterhofer: We worked! The day started on site at 9 am at the latest. It got unbearably hot in the course of the day. We'd stay there until around 7 pm, just before it got dark. Then we would shower, have dinner together and go to bed relatively early.

What was the building site like? And who was on site?
Martin Mitterhofer: On site were us students and the locals – the workers who helped us. Some of them were apprentices, some professional workers, some only laborers. Then there were the security guards, who liked to watch what was going on. At the beginning, there were sometimes more than 100 people on site. It was completely packed. But this normalized with time. There were "supervisors" from the group of local helpers, who assigned the workers to jobs.

Did you work together with the people?

Helena Brückner: Without the large number of workers, we wouldn't have managed to complete the project within the short period of time. They helped us with harvesting bamboo, with building, and with digging the foundation. Initially, there was some reserve, of course, but friendships soon developed and finally it was heart-breaking when we went back home.

Martin Mitterhofer: I was part of the bamboo team. There were two workers in the team who watched us building. Our assistants had previously trained us, and we passed on our skills, so to speak. The workers sometimes took notes and made drawings. We tried to create a collaboration without hierarchies, but the hierarchies are already in their heads. We were addressed as "boss," for example, even though we were at least 15 years younger. We tried to change this, and sometimes it worked.

Shpresa Cekaj: I was mainly responsible for things related to steel. For example, I tied up the entire building with a ring beam together with two local workers, who first had to show me how to do it, and then we continued together. I merely specified the lengths for them. The workers were quite surprised that we weren't fully trained. It was also difficult to explain to them what architects do, since this profession doesn't exist there in the same form.

How did you feel?

Shpresa Cekaj: At the beginning, I was curious, but also very excited. None of us had ever built anything before! I was worried about doing things right and managing. After all, craftsmanship is a skill that has to be learned.

Moritz Klein: I found it incredibly exciting to work together with the locals on site. We connected on an entirely different level, since we worked and sweated together intensively. That's a completely different way of connecting with people.

Did your work on site meet your expectations or did everything turn out quite differently?

Helena Brückner: Since I come from Namibia, it did feel like two worlds were colliding, because I thought I knew Africa. But Sierra Leone is very different, very poor, very simple, there's relatively little infrastructure, no running water, and no electricity. These are all areas that need to be developed.

Martin Mitterhofer: I had no expectations at all, as I'd never been exposed to a different culture group before. Of course I was nervous, but that was mainly due to the many vaccinations, to be honest. I felt like I needed to protect myself from something. That did cause a bit of insecurity. But apart from that, every day had a surprise in store for me.

In what way?

Martin Mitterhofer: I was surprised by the people's love of life despite the great poverty. There's not much money really. Everybody provides for themselves, and despite the very simple conditions people are cheerful, optimistic, and highly creative. There's a lot to learn from them — and from their techniques, too. There was a good exchange in many areas.

Moritz Klein: It was rather extreme to be confronted with the situation there. No running water, just from the well, the electricity was produced by generators only, and most food items were imported. This made us realize how high our standard of living and consumption are.

The design was initially developed at TUM. How did the design process go?
Helena Brückner: Several designs were produced during the first semester and one of them was selected. An execution plan was then developed by a smaller group in the second semester.
Franziska Odametey: We planned the building in every detail from foundation to roof and thought about materials and connections.

◄
Installation of the oven in which the bamboo sticks are smoked

Building the outer wall of the school

▲
Part of the already erected school building

Helena Brückner: Then we had regular meetings with our tutors and Professor Hermann Kaufmann. It became more and more detailed. We even took part in a brickmaking course in the end. So we learned how to make bricks at university!
Franziska Odametey: It was not possible to realize all the plans 1:1. We didn't look at the plans much at the building site, because many things turned out completely different in the end. Of course the basic things were realized according to plan, but we had to change the roof construction immediately after our arrival, for example. That was quite frustrating, since we had invested so much time. We had to get used to the idea that the building just looks a little differ-

ent here and there, but altogether, we're all very pleased.

And internally? What was it like to design together as a group?
Martin Mitterhofer: Surprisingly good! Sure, we were nine students, so there were always nine opinions formed by nine minds. Everybody thinks and experiences architecture in a different way. There was the occasional argument and slammed door. But then, we'd have a beer, and everything was alright again. In the end, we were a family. We still meet up today.
Moritz Klein: The design phase can certainly push you to your limits. Of course, it's a completely different story when nine people design together instead of just two. Two people also

have issues, but a consensus is reached at some point. This gets more difficult with nine people. It's impossible for so many people to have the same opinion about a design. There are endless discussions, much too long about some things for sure. But these discussions are simply necessary to bring everybody on board. It was certainly emotionally exhausting. It's hard to make so many compromises after having spent a lot of time on the design. That's not always easy. But when the building works afterwards, it's all the nicer when many people were involved. I like this kind of design process, even though I wonder whether the situa-

tion of nine participants with an equal say will ever happen again. Ultimately, there's something from each of us in it, and it really helps to achieve a lot, especially when working out the details. Everyone is needed in order to manage the volume in such a short space of time later. There's probably no way of realizing such projects other than in a bottom-up democratic fashion.

In what ways do DesignBuild projects such as this one differ from the other design seminars offered at the university?
Shpresa Cekaj: We usually work on a project. We develop a building task, then a spatial program,

and after that we deal with the design. Sometimes we build models and take photos of them. Often we also create 3D models. We add all the details to the drawing and picture the result in our minds. Seeing the ideas and drawings realized 1:1 is however something that normally doesn't happen.

Are you happy with the result?
Helena Brückner: Yes, definitely. When I stood in the courtyard and in front of our buildings for the first time and saw the paths and building lines, I felt very satisfied. Sure, when studying architecture, you learn from the beginning how a foundation works, what it looks like, and

what kind of distances must be observed. We can draw everything perfectly, but only get to see the plot at the construction site, and this one was very different regarding the heights. We had to excavate a bit more, and then, an unexpected foundation even appeared. So we had to rethink on site. And then you see all the people helping you, and how somehow everything works out and becomes an entity. You get to see how much work is involved, especially in countries like that without much construction machinery.

Martin Mitterhofer: I'm pleased with the design, but not with the result, since the school's still not ready for use. The reason for this certainly isn't the motivation of the local workers or the commitment of the students. The problem is that time pressure did not allow decisions to be changed once made – like building with bamboo, although we realized in the end that it wasn't possible to treat the material. We would never have taken such a risk with a project in Germany. The problem is now being resolved retroactively, and I hope that the school will be ready for use soon.

How did the people there react?
Martin Mitterhofer: At the beginning they didn't understand the design very well. We also didn't bring any illustrations with us. In fact, it took some time for it to be accepted. I'm sure there still are some locals who disapprove of the building, who consider the rooms, their layout, and their uses to be illogical. The complex is indeed quite different from the school-

houses that are usually built there. We arranged the classrooms around a courtyard. This design type was completely new to them. They don't know any schools with rooms for independent learning or practicing just for the students, for instance. It's commonplace for us, but there, it was a new concept.
Shpresa Cekaj: Many people were wondering what we were up to, because they didn't understand the large floor plans and sections. In order to understand constructions by looking at the plans, you need to have studied or understand architecture. We kept being asked things like why the roof had to end just there and didn't offer protection from the rain because of that. We tried to answer all these questions. Once the walls were high enough to give an idea of what the building would look like, everyone was very impressed, especially by the bamboo construction. One man said that he'd never seen such a design in Sierra Leone before. It was something

completely new to him and he was very proud to have been part of it. It might have been better to discuss the project with the people on site a bit earlier and explain it, what it looks like and why it looks like that. Then we would all have started with the same expectations.

On the whole, what didn't you like that much?
Helena Brückner: Communication should be improved to make it possible to move around the building site as equals, rather than to feel like we come from a more privileged cultural group for this reason alone. It would be better to spend more time there, not just show up, build something, and then leave. Many more workshops with the local community should be offered before starting these projects, so that we students can get to know the people there on a personal level and then develop the project together, not alone.
Franziska Odametey: I also found it hard that we hadn't been there before. We tried to

understand the needs of the local people, but then we went to Pepel and had to realize that their ideas and wishes are sometimes quite different. The exchange should have been more intensive. We should have found out more about what really matters. Also because of the completely different mentality. The people in Sierra Leone find things important that don't matter to us and vice versa.
Martin Mitterhofer: It was extremely difficult to develop a feeling without knowing the context and the people. I would also have liked to develop a communal design in regular consultation with the local people. More preparation is definitely needed. But I still found it good to be thrown in at the deep end. You learn a lot about the building site. That was really positive. But I wouldn't try putting up a building of that size within two months again. It also wouldn't have worked in this case, if all the participants hadn't worked ten-hour shifts for three weeks. This caused stress, and the we

and the workers got more and more exhausted. One could ask what's more important: the people or the project? Is it more important to finish the project, or is it about realizing it together? Without the proper framework conditions, I don't know whether I'd participate in such a project again, even though it was the best time of my life. I made friends and am still in touch with the people there. I also want to return, just to see what has happened since then. The people have grown close to our hearts. What I generally also find problematic is that projects are scattered around the continent. New locations crop up all the time. In my opinion, it would be more sustainable to be able to focus on one community and build up or develop something there.
Moritz Klein: I would also have liked to have more time. Everything had to be completed in just eight weeks, otherwise the project would have failed, since there were many things that depended on our presence on site. There

also wasn't a plan B. This created enormous pressure and great dependence issues. It would be better to have neither. The constraints resulting from this need to be prevented.

◄
Bamboo cutting for the roof

Wall construction with loam bricks (adobe)

▲
Loam brick (adobe) walls

Construction of the roof structure with bamboo

What did you particularly like?
Shpresa Cekaj: Working in such a big group and experiencing the dynamics behind it. I also liked the division into different trades. At the beginning, I had to find my own place and see what I'm good at. I'd return to the construction site without hesitation. To me, the most important part was working together with the people.

Moritz Klein: There was emotional support within the group. That was very important and a source of energy on the building site. Ultimately, we only made it that far because we all worked together. For me, it was an important experience to actually realize a building — from the theoretical ideas in the workroom to the building site and the constructional solutions that had to be found. It was a tremendous learning curve for me to understand how architecture is realized, the concessions that have to be made, which things change, and what constraints there are.

Was it hard to come back?
Martin Mitterhofer: For me, going away was not difficult. You just hop on a plane; but arriving was hard. It was a unique experience, to work together with the locals every day and be part of their culture. There's no other way of traveling that allows such fast immersion.

Helena Brückner: The arrival was crazy! We had really adapted our style of living. Everything was so simple, and we realized that you don't need much at all. We got used to a very simple rhythm of life. The worries we have here didn't exist there, and in Germany you suddenly realize: Wow, there's so many things here. Do we really need this overabundance? They are certainly two different worlds, but it was great to have had this experience. The time in Sierra Leone broadened my horizon.

Limits

URSULA HARTIG

DesignBuild is becoming increasingly successful in architecture and engineering science courses. More and more universities and universities of applied sciences offer projects aiming to produce built objects as outcomes. This is confirmed by the predominantly good performance of participants reflected in corresponding grades, and the number of student admissions and establishment of Master and postgraduate degree courses[1] despite the difficulty of appropriately adapting existing curricular structures, which is only achievable through compromise by lecturers and students. Projects are gaining increasing visibility in public architectural discourse; they are publicized and awarded prizes in competition with professional architectural offices.

Their realization means that DesignBuild projects leave the scope of a classical architectural education, and even go far beyond the conventional services included in an architectural contract. Instead, they resemble the performance expected from a full-service general contractor: project acquisition, basic evaluation, planning and building services, construction above ground, support structure planning, landscape and garden construction, installations and often also financing are frequently completed by DesignBuild studios and their management.

These services are required to fulfill specifications – both from within and without – regarding participative planning methods, social relevance, effectiveness and fairness, intercultural/international exchange, economic acceptability, technical and design-related innovation, and sustainability – and yet these projects are primarily for academic training purposes, often embedded in a research context. Focus is on the process rather than on the product.

Learning from mistakes is a valuable experience. Research should be experimental, innovative, and with an open outcome – the result does not necessarily have to be as expected or desired. Since DesignBuild is used as an educational method, there must also be room for errors and failure in such projects. In her contribution to a conference on the subject DesignBuild, Tolya Stonorov has stated that the possibility of making errors must be part of the DesignBuild practice and that there is much to learn from failures.[2] Errors that may lead to the failure of a project are, however, not acceptable in projects that give people reason to hope for an improvement of their living situation.

DesignBuild projects in fact bear a broad range of incalculable risks and barely foreseeable obstacles. However, critical discourse is rare and mainly limited to a description of challenges and how these were ultimately mastered. Project evaluations, long-term studies or at least medium-term documentations providing information about success and – more importantly – failure, are not readily available. This is understandable, since these complex projects are subject to demands and criticism from many sides while they are still in the process of establishing themselves in academic education.[3]

Kitchen in the Jam manufactory for Naxiít, a project in San Gerónimo Tecoatl, Mexico by TU Berlin, completed in April 2012, picture taken in March 2019

PROJECT PROCESS

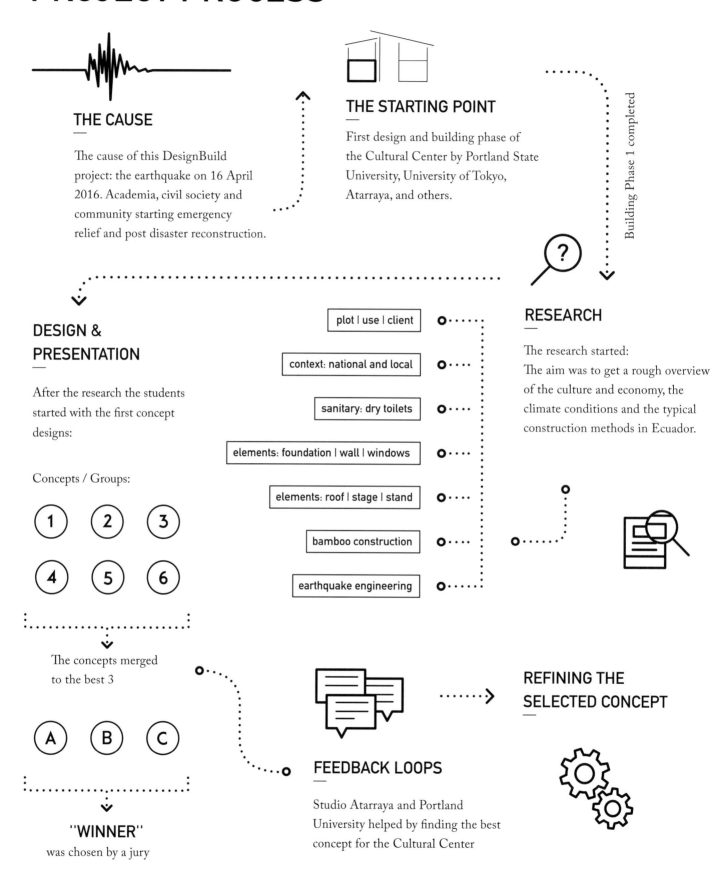

THE CAUSE

The cause of this DesignBuild project: the earthquake on 16 April 2016. Academia, civil society and community starting emergency relief and post disaster reconstruction.

THE STARTING POINT

First design and building phase of the Cultural Center by Portland State University, University of Tokyo, Atarraya, and others.

Building Phase 1 completed

DESIGN & PRESENTATION

After the research the students started with the first concept designs:

Concepts / Groups:

1   2   3

4   5   6

The concepts merged to the best 3

A   B   C

"WINNER"
was chosen by a jury

plot | use | client

context: national and local

sanitary: dry toilets

elements: foundation | wall | windows

elements: roof | stage | stand

bamboo construction

earthquake engineering

RESEARCH

The research started:
The aim was to get a rough overview of the culture and economy, the climate conditions and the typical construction methods in Ecuador.

FEEDBACK LOOPS

Studio Atarraya and Portland University helped by finding the best concept for the Cultural Center

REFINING THE SELECTED CONCEPT

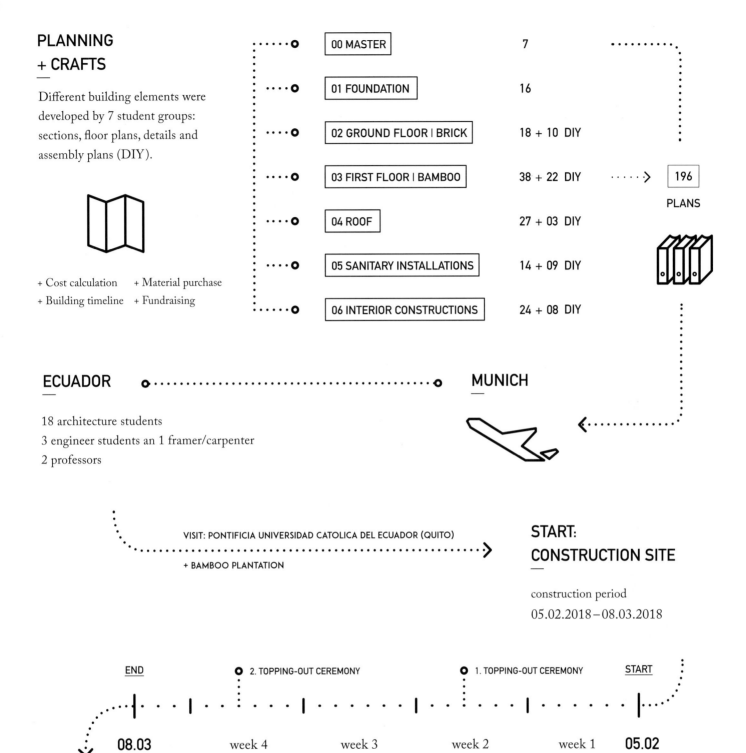

PLANNING
+ CRAFTS

Different building elements were
developed by 7 student groups:
sections, floor plans, details and
assembly plans (DIY).

+ Cost calculation   + Material purchase
+ Building timeline   + Fundraising

00 MASTER	7	
01 FOUNDATION	16	
02 GROUND FLOOR	BRICK	18 + 10 DIY	
03 FIRST FLOOR	BAMBOO	38 + 22 DIY	196 PLANS
04 ROOF	27 + 03 DIY	
05 SANITARY INSTALLATIONS	14 + 09 DIY	
06 INTERIOR CONSTRUCTIONS	24 + 08 DIY	

ECUADOR

18 architecture students
3 engineer students an 1 framer/carpenter
2 professors

MUNICH

VISIT: PONTIFICIA UNIVERSIDAD CATOLICA DEL ECUADOR (QUITO)

+ BAMBOO PLANTATION

START:
CONSTRUCTION SITE

construction period
05.02.2018 – 08.03.2018

END   2. TOPPING-OUT CEREMONY   1. TOPPING-OUT CEREMONY   START

08.03   week 4   week 3   week 2   week 1   **05.02**

WORKING TIME

4.5 weeks = 28 days
= 280 h = 16,800 min

MATERIALS

concrete + steel + wood + bamboo
+ brick + clay

STUDIO
CHAMANGA

RESEARCH DESIGN BUILD

Only successful DesignBuild projects are presented and discussed in conferences, publications, and exhibitions. Like in professional architecture, well-illuminated photographs of recently completed buildings or making-of pictures of students swinging axes are used to woo observers and critics. Essentially reduced to the projects' visual appearance at the moment of completion, this documentation (though important for many reasons) can neither reflect the complexity of the projects nor make an authoritative statement on their quality. At best, it serves to confirm adherence to a budget and timeline as well as a specific spatial-architectural quality – to the degree of what is distinguishable in the images. At worst, the documentation disguises failure at other levels.[4]

In addition to buildings, the DesignBuild projects create – purposely or unintentionally – a large spectrum of immaterial, hard to depict results. After all, each of the actors involved in the projects has their own agenda: user groups and building owners, sponsors and financial backers, government and non-government organizations, university managements, craftsmen, students, lecturers, and researchers working in different disciplines and countries, and many more. The effect is not always positive for everyone and not all the actors concerned are in a position to complain.

In contrast to professional projects, the relationship between principal and agent is not an economic one, since the service is not remunerated by payment. A user group is faced with planners and builders who, moreover, often provide the financial means for the project, essentially gifting it; in this respect, the acceptance and support of the project is in itself already a huge return service. Features normally forming the basis of a contract, such as a guaranteed absence of faults in the sense of a warranty, are therefore not applicable. Building errors do not result in penalties, and decisions regarding the design are often made far from realistic usage, in spite of participative requirements.

There are no regulations or binding quality criteria. The DesignBuild team normally has the decision-making power due to the donor-recipient imbalance as well as sociocultural differences, which leads to an ethical conflict. Users and building owners who provide the experimental ground for these trials have to bear the possible negative effects. "Too often, good intentions by novice designers place design over community needs. They impose projects onto communities by prioritizing design challenges and self-serving gains from awards and publications; then disappear, leaving the community with a structure without any input or position of ownership."[5]

Admitting mistakes, as well as their critical review and discussion, must form part of the academic DesignBuild culture in order to reduce negative effects of future projects on local communities and cooperation partners

◄◄
Diagram for project by Studio Chamanga Research Design Build, in Chamanga, Ecuador

Stage for the Rodolfo Morelos Music School in Ocotlan de Morelos 2015 during a workshop visit.

and to counteract an apparent naivety in handling user-related DesignBuild projects. It helps to define criteria and priorities in order to identify successful projects and make decisions. Beyond formal architectural criteria, framework conditions regarding the dimension and quality of the construction, durability, possibility, and necessity of maintenance as well as resistance to influences of nature must be specified. Most of all, it is important to clarify and agree on expectations and responsibilities with regard to resources, performance, and skills of the parties involved both before and in the course of the project. While changes and alterations in the agreed range of services are normal in such projects, they need to be designated as possible risks and communicated. Errors are intrinsic to science and research. Experimenting with the hardship and needs of people, however, provokes an ethical dilemma.

The aims and success criteria of projects, especially when a social impact is intended, must be defined and adapted carefully and transparently by all actors and interest groups, since the process and product have a huge impact on the life and surroundings of these persons. Failure is not an option here!

But what is also necessary is a discussion on limiting the responsibilities of the projects' protagonists, and hence on the limits of the complexity, knowledge, and skills that can be provided by a faculty of architecture and engineering in order to successfully and sustainably realize DesignBuild projects in the long term.

Ursula Hartig has been Professor for Planning and Building in a Global Context at the Munich University of Applied Sciences (MUAS) since 2017. She graduated from TU Berlin with the degree of Diplom Ingenieur. Since 1987, she has been a staff member and project leader in various architectural practices in Berlin. In 1997, she became a research associate at the Department of Architecture at TU Berlin. Since 2001, she has been in charge of DesignBuild studios at TU Berlin, including the planning, realization and documentation of buildings and surroundings in Mexico and Afghanistan. In 2004, she founded CoCoon – contextual construction, a DesignBuild project initiative that combines sustainable and contextual building with social commitment and intercultural exchange of knowledge.

1 Kunstuniversität Linz, basehabitat http://www.basehabitat.org/postgrad (accessed 21 November 2019).

2 Tolya Stonorov, "The Nest: Failure as a Pedagogical Model for Learning," in: *Working while Building III; Issues in DesignBuild: Learning from Failure,* Web Conference 2018.

3 "Why do the projects all look the same?"; "You are taking work away from the architects like that"; "You should also cooperate with sociologists, landscape architects, building services engineers and"; "Why aren't the students from the partner country involved in the planning?"; "You are taking work away from the people on location"; "You are introducing money and techniques in contexts that cannot handle them"; "You are exhibiting neocolonial behavior"; "The money spent by the students on flights would be enough to build three schools"; "We don't even get our administration involved for such a small sum"; "They are supposed to become architects, not craftsmen," etc.

4 Ursula Hartig, "Learning from Failure," in: Jane Anderson (ed.), *Architecture Connects – Association of Architectural Educators 4th International Peer Reviewed Conference, Oxford Brookes University, UK 6–9 September 2017 Proceedings*, Oxford 2017. https://aaeconference2017.wordpress.com/about-2/ (accessed 21 November 2019).

5 Anna Lee Koosmann about the project: Estudio Damgo III: A Filipino Design+Build Studio. Website of funding organization of project supported by a monitoring system ("Estudio Damgo III: A Filipino Design+Build Studio," n.y.). Global-Giving (accessed 07 October 2019). https://www.globalgiving.org/projects/estudiodamgo3/; Anna Lee Koosmann, "When Bold Design Can Lead to Build Blunders: Lessons on Design-Build Failure," in: Web Conference 2018.

Stage for the Rodolfo Morelos Music School in Ocotlan de Morelos shortly after its completion in 2008. The designBuild project was under the direction of the author.

On the DesignBuild Method

Creating high-quality and relevant architecture with Design-Build projects is a form-finding challenge as well as an extremely complex task in the design process. In contrast to the chronological structure of conventional projects, DesignBuild projects have a network-like structure with various planning and realization phases, and – enhanced by diverse actors in collaborative processes – meander from one development step to the next. This iterative method allows a successive solidification of important insights and requirements that the projects are to fulfill. A clear attitude (regarding design), robust concepts, and extensive design processes are essential to steering such a transformative and flexible process. These display an experimental (i.e. laboratory-like) character that is necessary for the development of precisely tailored architecture.

The overall objective is to create places and spaces that satisfy the highest architectural standards as well as acting as social catalysts. The onus is clearly on us – qualified architects and professors at the university – to take the lead in order to achieve this. This basically means that students are actively involved in all phases of the project, while the quality of the projects is defined and safeguarded by professional guidance. Rather than serving to develop the self-awareness of students, DesignBuild projects at CODE are therefore projects in which students learn to develop an individual architectural approach, with the aim of fulfilling the highest architectural standards. Students are part of a holistic process in which they not only design, plan, and realize, but also learn to understand the significance of architecture and its role in specific contexts. Our DesignBuild projects are in fact intended to make a real contribution to building *culture!*

◀ Agriculture and boarding school Bella Vista in the Andes of Bolivia. Designed and implemented by architecture students from the TU Berlin in the field of design and construction under the direction of Professor Ralf Pasel

Ralf Pasel is Professor for Design and Construction Technologies | CODE at TU Berlin and founding partner of Pasel.Künzel Architects in Rotterdam, Berlin, Munich. He has worked on experimental construction in an international context for many years. He has taught at various universities all over the world, including Pontificia Universidad Católica de Chile in Santiago, TU Delft, and Rotterdam Academy of Architecture and Urban Design.

Reflections on the Assessment

TOMÀ BERLANDA

DesignBuild is here understood as a pedagogical project at architectural institutions in which, for the first time, students implement one of their own design and learn how the built result may influence the individuals and communities it is intended for. The built objects, so the thesis of this contribution, must be questioned in a self-reflective way. To this end, the evaluation of the results and their impact should become an intrinsic step of the entire design process, which could be described as "thinking while working."

If in principle this is a largely shared position, in reality, for most Design-Build experiences the assessment is either the phase mostly left aside, or almost solely concerned with the ability to provide a positive learning experience to students. The growing dissatisfaction with the appropriateness of such evaluation methods has solicited reflections by some scholars, and attempts have been made to establish criteria which might help to overcome a piecemeal case-by-case approach. However, this is a process that is still underway.

To mention but one example, faculty at the University of Ljubljana embarked on a comparative analysis of a series of projects, to show "the scope, engagement, and the achieved outcome of the action,"[1] based on the following set of criteria: cooperation and involvement (with other higher education institutions, community, industry, nonprofit organizations); spatial level (local, regional, or international); project duration; the addressed issue (design problems, social issues, ecological aspect, multi-aspect approach); and the achieved outcome (valued, above all, on the basis of the achieved technical result).

Even though the intention to identify a set of comparable criteria is undoubtedly positive, it is worth remarking that the achieved outcomes are assessed in terms of technical results of the architectural object, and not in terms of the impact on its users. In other words, "how architecture is" continues to be considered more relevant than "what architecture does".

Challenges and needs (or the argument for an assessment)

Before offering some thoughts on what might be included in the assessment phase, a limited number of factual challenges are worth mentioning. If to determine and judge the value of something it is necessary to adopt objective, quantifiable, and comparable metrics, the evaluation of any architectural project is very difficult, since subjective criteria like the aesthetic appearance easily prevail.

Programmatic limitations and distance

DesignBuild projects are prevalently concerned with themes and sectors, such as health, education, and shelter, which are not interesting to the real estate market. The DesignBuilders thus end up replacing what in a less unjustly structured society should be taken care of by the public

◀
Community workshop for the Tacloban Design-Build project in Leyte, Philippines

sector. It is true that universities are public institutions to a varying degree, but the independence with which they are allowed to operate, particularly far away from their home country, in support of communities in distress, can sometimes be harmful, since there might be no regulatory system in place to control their operations. This condition would suggest making even more stringent the need of focusing the assessment on the effects that the existence of the built work and the activities to be housed will have on the living conditions of its users, rather than on the aesthetic qualities of the architectural piece.

Need to move beyond rhetorical language

It's hard not to notice how DesignBuild is a type of intervention increasingly becoming a field of privileged interest for academic institutions competing with one another, as evidenced by the self-celebrative language used to magnify their good intentions. Statements such as "the initiative continues to serve the poor in Asia, Latin America, Africa, and the USA and improve the lives of communities worldwide typically underserved"[2] and descriptions of "students, under the guidance of mentors, plan and build schools, kindergartens, and other social institutions in economically neglected countries, helping to address the spatial and life hardships of the population"[3] sound like hollow descriptors of what could be easily perceived as a missionary approach.

Thanks to the growing circulation of interventions of so-called humanitarian architecture, and of networks that join together practitioners and educators who share a belief that "we can create better environmental, social, and economic outcomes for all through the power of design," teachers and universities gain popularity and visibility, their projects capture the attention of magazines and media, and publications and awards specifically aimed at DesignBuild projects keep growing. The website ArchDaily now organizes the competitions for the best student's DesignBuild projects worldwide, and in 2012 ACSA, the American Association of Collegiate Schools of Architecture established the Design-Build Award. This new attention has two sides. On the one hand, it certainly serves to convince students and sponsors for the projects, but also the universities, since the teaching method is by no means self-evident and the teachers are usually in more precarious employment conditions. On the other hand, one must be careful that attention through various public media and awards does not contribute to an unreflective display of DesignBuild projects, where they are portrayed as "exquisite"[4] or "poetic"[5] structures.

Taking this skewed situation into consideration, it should not come as a surprise that the majority of the assessments end up being made up of cursory compliments stemming from the idea that a "good architecture for the poor" entails building quickly, using available and inexpensive

Safe Haven Library, Ban
Tha Song Yang, Thailand

materials, and the use of local low-cost labour,[6] and potentially offering an interpretation of the lessons of vernacular architecture.

Authors as assessors, no post-occupancy evaluation

A third challenge stems from the fact that the judgement on the project is expressed immediately after the completion of the works, and hence not much can be said on how much the needs that the design intended to address were indeed satisfied. The lack of any medium or long-term post-occupancy assessment is detrimental to the critical reflection on what did in fact work. This hurdle is compounded by the fact that the assessment is carried out by the same designers and authors. However animated by good intentions they might be, it is understandable that they are prone to positively evaluate their experience, resulting in the role of the beneficiaries of the schemes becoming inexistent in the assessment.

Positive experiences

Not all operate in the same way. Some faculty involved in the Design-Build experiences are well aware of the reasons that make it difficult to develop adequate assessment procedures and have addressed this both from a theoretical point of view and by elaborating and experimenting with a range of different criteria.

Perhaps for this reason the most convincing attempts are the ones by institutions who have engaged with DesignBuild courses over multiple iterations and have chosen to operate in close proximity to their premises. The ensuing projects are therefore not isolated initiatives but part of a consolidated relationship between the university and a community.

One such instance is that of Rural Studio at the University of Alabama, where old projects are evaluated with the beginning of each new semester, and only after considering the feedback from the individuals using the building, a new initiative is launched. It is an attitude that is possibly conceptually tied to the ethical approach described by the founder of the studio Samule Mockbee, who theorized the "leadership of the architect"and stated how the architectural profession had "an ethical responsibility to help improve living conditions for the poor".[7]

A tentative list

In order to bring the discussion full circle, what follows is a sequence of points that should be kept in mind when establishing both a baseline for evaluation and a lens through which to look at the results.

1. Include from the beginning

The first suggestion is to include the evaluation procedure as part of the initial briefing, together with a clear framing of needs, interests, and expectations. This would mitigate the risk that an ex-post assessment might end up privileging a choice of vague criteria and result in approximate measures. The final report should further respond to the initial framing of the pedagogical assignment, and extend the observations beyond the qualities of the architectural object as such, by taking into consideration procedures and outcomes.

2. How does the encounter between the designers and the client take place

"Who chooses whom" is a question that cannot be left unanswered in a historical moment where organizations specializing in the choice

Construction of counter for the restaurant, Øst-markneset, Trondheim, Norway, 2015

of communities "eligible" to receive help appear to be growing. Today the promoters of the initiatives are not alone in establishing precise selection criteria. Indeed, there are networks of Western architectural faculties purposely created for the construction of public buildings in developing countries and institutions today that are specialized in project management.

3. Who decides the brief and who chooses the project conformance to specification of the brief

In the reports from DesignBuild activities, rhetorical echoes of participation and inclusion of the local population abound, even though this involvement pivots around an uneven relation between creator and fabricator. Indeed, it is no longer possible to shy away from contributing to the conversation on how, in practice, to apply the overarching criterion demanding that the community affected by our work must participate in the planning of the intervention and not be left to be consulted in the ex-post evaluation.

4. Who decides the financial allocation

Besides the financial contributions of donors and sponsors it should be clearly indicated how the labor of local inhabitants is valued and quantified, in order to avoid conveying a message of simply extracting wealth from communities.

5. Time

From a temporal point of view, it would be beneficial to identify for each group the immediate short-term outcomes, which generally are the most well-documented and publicized, intermediate outcomes, such as challenges in the maintenance and running of the facility, and ultimate longer-term outcomes, such as use of the structure, potential changes and modifications brought to the building, as well as replicability.

6. Context

Concerning location, the assessment should be understood in terms of the site and the context where the project is implemented, making a distinction between designs built in places and for users close to the academic institutions, or in underprivileged settings, and between episodic projects and those which are part of a lasting relationship between universities and local communities.

7. Users' satisfaction

The satisfaction of the users' needs, besides being difficult to measure, is easily manipulated, and even more so in the case of projects carried out in distant locations and across varying conditions of social and economic discomfort.

8. Specific skills or knowledge transfer

On this point, designers generally do not shy away from the myth of knowledge exchange and tend to underline as a positive result that of having taught the locals how to build in an appropriate way. Clear, measurable parameters should be developed to mitigate the one-directionality of the approach.

9. Changed attitudes or values about specific issues and modified behavior

All designers agree on the idea that the experience of building a project in a foreign context by one's own hand not only broadened their cultural horizon but increased their professional competence. The impact of their activities on the behavior and positions of the inhabitants of the Global South is a theme rarely taken into consideration. Greater attention to the changes that the designs have brought to the local population is possible in the case of projects realized in close proximity to the initiating universities. The goal of "engaging with people as equals" and promoting "new forms of coexistence" is explicit in designs where, besides academia, also citizens, the administration, and notprofit organizations are involved in the construction. The challenge in this approach is to emphasize a communicative learning model that both draws on the local context and empowers its population.

Conversion of a building dating back to World War II into a restaurant. The project originates from the Østmarkneset workshop by NTNU Live Studio, Trondheim Norway, 2015

1   Branislav Folić, Saja Kosanović, Tadej Glažar, Alenka Fikfak, "Design-Build Concept In Architectural Education," 2016. https://www.academia.edu/32503899/Design-Build_Concept_In_Architectural_Education (accessed 30 November 2019).

2   http://www.centerforpublicinterestdesign.org/people (accessed 30 November 2019)

3   http://www.ugm.si/en/stara-stran/news-4/?tx_news_pi1%5Bnews%5D=3321&tx_news_pi1%5Bcontroller%5D=News&tx_news_pi1%5Baction%5D=detail&cHash=5900a5b77e7c2464287c1f35ea8b77ab (accessed 30 November 2019).

4   https://design-build.space/awards (accessed 30 November 2019).

5   https://www.scandinaviandesign.com/the-erskine-award-2017/ (accessed 30 November 2019).

6   https://www.uni-lj.si/news/news/5213/ (accessed 30 November 2019)

7   Michael Hensel, "Rural Studio: Incarnations of a Design and Build Programme," 2015. https://onlinelibrary.wiley.com/doi/abs/10.1002/ad.1875 n (accessed 30 November 2019).

Tomà Berlanda is Professor of Architecture at the School of Architecture, Planning and Geomatics at the University of Cape Town. His research interests focus on the implications that can be drawn from a non-stereotypical reading of the African city and the practice of architecture in non-Western urban settings and landscapes. He co-founded asa studio and astudio.space, two practices that have produced internationally recognized design work. His collaborative projects are the result of an engagement with the role of quality design for underprivileged communities and includes school buildings, early childhood development centers, and health facilities. He is the author of *Architectural Topographies* (Routledge, Abington 2014), and *Interpreting Kigali* (University of Arkansas Press, Fayetteville, AR 2018) and served as Technical Reviewer for the Aga Khan Award for Architecture in 2016 and 2019.

What Should We Have for Dinner Tonight…?

The Auburn University Rural Studio academic program, inspired by founder Samuel Mockbee's deep knowledge of the place, provides answers to questions or situations that evolve over time; answers unique to the place, its community, and the ever-evolving needs of society at large. The Rural Studio academic program concerns itself with place, architecture, and society, all three of which are in a continuous state of flux.

The place is the connecting thread linking Rural Studio projects, but their evolution cannot be fully understood without appreciating the importance of the knowledge transfer from one project to the next, year in, year out. Every project is in some way the result of the experience, mistakes, and successes of all previous projects.

Each project is a response to (or a dialogue with) the place, in a moment in time. A project is always a manifesto, an architectural answer to a particular situation.

Our primary mission is to educate future architects.
We work in an underserved rural community, in the west of Alabama.
We ask ourselves many questions.

What should be built instead of what can we build?
How can we better prepare our students?
What should they learn?
What should they take from this experience?
How do we have to build in rural areas in this moment in time?
Which projects will impact the community more?
How can we better use our resources?
Is there a different way to think about everyday life?
Are there new ways of understanding work and production that are more appropriate to our place?

Maybe, in a simpler way, we just need to ask ourselves, regardless of which discipline we are in: How should we live now, what is the best use of our resources, and what should we have for dinner tonight…?

◄
Fire station in Newbern,
built by students from
the Rural Studio at
Auburn University, 2004

Xavier Vendrell studied architecture in his native city of Barcelona, where he has been practicing architecture since 1983. His work embraces a wide range of scales from landscape architecture and urban design to public buildings, housing, and interior design. In 1999, Xavier Vendrell founded Xavier Vendrell Studio Chicago/Barcelona, a collaborative practice for architecture, landscape, and design. He has been a professor at UIC Barcelona School of Architecture and at University of Illinois at Chicago School of Architecture. From 2002 to 2012, he was a consultant for Rural Studio, Auburn University. Since 2013, he has been a professor at the Rural Studio, where he was Acting Director from 2016 to 2018.

Form Follows Needs – DesignBuild from the Perspective of an Architectural Psychologist

TANJA C. VOLLMER

Form follows needs. This version of the expression "form follows function" coined by the American architect Louis Sullivan in 1896,[1] can be used to sum up the approach of the DesignBuild teaching method. In direct contact with users and clients, craftsmen and construction equipment, stones and steel girders, students get to know the essence of what should at best be the result of an architectural effort: a building. At the same time, they explore the reality of a process characterized by miscellaneous and complex requirements. Quite often, the ideas and wishes of those ultimately using the building differ from those of the client, which inevitably places the architect in the role of a change manager. Craftsmen have routines that are hard to break and materials have inherent properties with sometimes unpredictable consequences. The architect then necessarily switches from the role of creator of a spatial composition to that of a coach, material scientist, and crisis manager. By dealing with actual problems during the realization of their design, students are familiarized with the underlying needs of the relevant factors – both subjective and objective. They practise strategies to learn to handle them and cooperate to finally find a joint solution. Pedagogy describes this process as problem-oriented learning (POL).[2] DesignBuild however goes even further. Problems are not constructed or simulated, but occur quite naturally through the demand for realization. They prompt the students to critically reflect on their designs and any resulting adaptations. Important skills such as social interaction and empathy, conflict resolution behavior, and exploration are practiced in the quest for solutions – apart from purely technical and craftsmanship-related abilities. "Building is not my trade [...] but one should know it!" commented the Dutch architect and Professor of Design, Francine Houben, on the teaching method at TU Delft in 2016.[3] In purely academically taught design, the only design critic is normally a professor who pushes the design projects ahead by subjecting the students to a series of reflective revision loops. In DesignBuild, the professor is replaced by several non-academic critics who assess the design

on the basis of their needs-driven expertise. Apart from the positive learning effects mentioned above, this transformation and simultaneous externalization of the critical spirit into a kind of practical rationality, however, also bears a risk that should not be underestimated.

Going back to the time of the church father Augustine (354–430), whose teaching was based on the idea that bodies cannot be comprehended by the mind and that physical things are only perceptible through the senses, DesignBuild assumes that architectural students need the sensory perception of the surroundings, material, and people in order to understand the spatial structures created by themselves. Moreover, this understanding will only be possible through an execution of their design in interaction with people, machines, and material. This principle was contradicted vehemently by Thomas Aquinas's five questions regarding intellectual insight back in the 13th century. After all, one cannot touch the water of a fast-flowing river twice in the same place – so his interpretation of Heraclitus.[4] Architects cannot experience and touch the material being used every time before they consider it to be in the right place of their design. Neuroscientific findings of the 21st century agree with Aquinas. When we think about a specific object, it doesn't make any difference at all to our brain whether we are standing right in front of it or sitting in a comfortable chair. In 1969, the German-American psychologist Rudolf Arnheim described this phenomenon as "visual thinking". "The cognitive operations called thinking are not the privilege of mental processes above and beyond perception, but the essential ingredients of perception itself."[5] And furthermore, only when the mind considers its own requirements as satisfied or unsatisfied by the nature of things does it actually grasp their properties. "Rather than being detached from us objectively – like a thing – architectural space is interactional. It is intended to allow people to relate to each other mentally, socially, and culturally as well as to relate to their tangible world,"[6] explained Wolfgang Meisenheimer in his book *Das Denken des Leibes und der architektonische Raum* (Physical Thinking and Architectural Space). Louis Sullivan, famous for his early monolithic skyscrapers, followed this credo. Instead of regarding ornamentation as a decorative art, for example, he considered it solely to fulfill the function of satisfying the deepest human need for identification with the immediate environment – he assumed that no human beings could recognize themselves in something that was honed smooth. Bauhaus representatives, on the other hand, tried to misinterpret his "form follows function" approach as functionalism. For DesignBuild, it is similarly very tempting to misinterpret "form follows needs" as utilitarianism of sensory perception. Students are allowed too little time and scope for preparation of the execution task to learn to master the instruments of a real needs analysis. This means that instead of needs, the requirements that are mainly identified and acted upon in the heat of the realization process are those that have already been preformulated by the client. Architectural psychology, as an integrative component of design studies, has lately been offering methods allowing needs analysis to be used effectively for design purposes at an early phase of concept development. This approach requires students to explore the causes and effects involved in the interaction between humans and the

Students observe the activities of their fellow students regarding the design in the dark.

environment. What makes us happy, healthy, active, considerate, or just? What supports, touches, warms, liberates, and inspires us? This means that, before they even come into contact with the diversity of concrete problems and requirements of the design, planning, and building process, students delve into a world that is ultimately responsible for the assessment of their creative act: human nature. Admittedly, this too is scientifically founded, but being anchored in ourselves allows the necessary scope for "dreaming."

While the realist and critic in and around the student receive adequate input, DesignBuild currently still leaves the dreamer by the wayside. Yet the dreamer is indispensable for architecture. The soberness with which designers fashion our environment nowadays is low-risk, because it enables them to evade critics. It is useful and functional, because it either doesn't allow problems to come to exist in the first place or makes it possible to solve them quickly. It most of all, however, mirrors a university education in which – from a psychological perspective – the needs of self-fulfillment, the ego-needs, and hence the dreamer in every student are subdued or at least significantly neglected. It is said that Walt Disney assumed three different consecutive roles in the course of his work: that of the dreamer, the realist, and the critic.[7] Disney consciously kept these roles as far apart as possible. Later he apparently even used three different rooms for his thinking modes. In the dreamer's space, he came up with fantastic ideas that played with possibilities, but mainly with impossibilities. Everything was allowed in this space, except to think about a concrete problem seriously. In the realist's space, he tried to develop the dreamer's idea and fit it into reality. Only in the critic's space did he subject himself to his own relentless criticism. Of exceptional significance in this regard was that he only focused on his own needs with this criticism. The connection of place and thinking mode is also decisive for the creative learning process in architectural and design studies. In the DesignBuild method, the change of place currently, however, still takes the form of a standardized problem-solving procedure, which the Maltese doctor and psychologist Edward de Bono describes as conducive to vertical thinking, in which one step of the solution follows the other consistently and systematically. This is contrasted by lateral or also divergent thinking. Divergent thinking goes back to the American psychologist and psychometrician Joy Paul Guilford and means approaching problems in an open, unsystematic, and playful manner.[8] In short, the opposite of a problem-oriented fixation on reality or of rational utilitarianism. An essential prerequisite for divergent thinking to be able to develop, is to switch off thinking barriers and critical reservations. DesignBuild students would therefore at this point have to turn their back on the construction site for a while and make room for paradoxical results to allow divergent thinking and the resultant creative solution to emerge. Despite the scepticism of modern cognitive psychology with regard to purely bilateral thinking theories, there is considerable approval as far as the validity in teaching creative design and production processes is concerned.

Such a cognitive-psychological consideration of design studies – as inherent in architectural psychology – naturally raises the ancient and still widely discussed question of the measure of creativity in architecture. Do we train artists, craftsmen, or technicians – or perhaps something in between? The positive DesignBuild learning targets stated at the beginning are undoubtedly a gain for academic architectural teaching. The consideration from an architectural-psychology perspective indicates that its potential as a modern method meeting the requirements of university-level academic thinking is not yet fully exploited. If DesignBuild manages to occupy the intersections

Tanja C. Vollmer is Visiting Professor of Architectural Psychology and Health Building Design at the Faculty of Architecture of TUM (Technical University of Munich). She completed her studies in Biology and Psychology at Georg-August University of Göttingen with a doctorate and obtained a Master in Health Psychology at Harvard Medical School in Boston, USA. From 2000 to 2006, she worked as Scientific Director of Psycho-Oncology at the hospital of the Ludwig Maximilian University of Munich; from 2016 to 2018 as Visiting Professor at TU Berlin. In addition, she is co-owner of the research and design office kopvol architecture & psychology in Rotterdam and Berlin. Vollmer researches and teaches with a focus on perceptual changes associated with severe and chronic illness and their impact on architecture. Her book *Die Erkrankung des Raumes* (Sickness of Space) (utzverlag, Munich 2010) set a standard for modern architectural psychology in health building design.

between psychology and architecture more effectively in the future, and if it allocates more scope and time to divergent thinking and needs analysis, it will, however, be able to safely accompany the new human-centered engineering approach as a teaching and learning method.

1 Louis H. Sullivan, "The Tall Office Building Artistically Considered," in: *Lippincott's Monthly Magazine* 3, 1896, pp. 403–409.

2 Cf. Kurt Reusser, "Problemorientiertes Lernen. Tiefenstruktur, Gestaltungsformen, Wirkung," in: *Beiträge zur Lehrerinnen- und Lehrerbildung* 23 (2), 2005, pp. 159–182.

3 Extracted from a presentation talk by Francine Houben on the competition design of the Princess Máxima Center for Paediatric Oncology, Utrecht 2011.

4 Thomas von Aquin, *Fünf Fragen über die intellektuelle Erkenntnis*, trans. Karl Borman, Hamburg reprint 1986.

5 Cf. Rudolf Arnheim, *Anschauliches Denken: Zur Einheit von Bild und Begriff,* German translation, Cologne 1996; published in English as *Visual Thinking,* Berkeley 1969.

6 Wolfgang Meisenheimer, *Das Denken des Leibes und der architektonische Raum*, Berlin 2004.

7 Cf. Richard Schickel, *Disneys Welt. Zeit, Leben, Kunst & Kommerz des Walt Disney*, German translation, Berlin 1997.
The Disney Version: The Life, Times, Art and Commerce of Walt Disney (1968); revised editions: 1984, 1997

8 Joy Paul Guilford: "Creativity," in: *American Psychologist*, Vol. 5, 1950, pp. 444–454.

Design Manifesto

The key criterion in initiating a DesignBuild project for students is to do with the learning opportunity. Further criteria are time schedules in the context of the academic calendar, the appropriate scale for students, and the flexibility and eagerness of clients or beneficiaries to work with a collective process involving students.

The main motivation for bringing such projects into academia is in allowing students to experience how the design process continues beyond the concept stage, into working drawings and cost estimates, and even during the execution of the project, in terms of decision-making on the smallest of details. Typically, formal architectural studies concentrate on arriving at a concept stage during a whole semester for all semesters, and students graduate without having to take their designs further by integrating technical aspects. Architectural education is incomplete if the curriculum does not include all stages of the architect's role. My main aim is to have the students encounter four ground realities and respond to these sensitively, aesthetically, and humanely: real scale, real materials, real people, and real place. Personal engagement with these real aspects that underpin architecture inspires good architecture.

The most valuable realization is that architecture is people-centric, made for people and by people, and a backdrop for human life to take place. DesignBuild projects allow students to engage in the process through personal interaction with geographical, historical, and climatic aspects. They also have the opportunity to test their knowledge of structures, geometry, material, and technologies and to develop a curiosity for seeking knowledge when confronted with their own limits. Developing the art of communication in the process is also key. Through presentations to clients and beneficiaries, consultants, contractors, or builders as well as within internal group processes, experiential learning takes place as an interdisciplinary collaborative process, entailing the development of social skills. This is bound to be empowering.

Anupama Kundoo, architect and professor at Potsdam School of Architecture, Germany, graduated in 1989 from Sir JJ College of Architecture, University of Mumbai, and received her PhD from the TU Berlin in 2008. Kundoo's practice, started in 1990, involves extensive material research and experimentation to achieve an architecture of low environmental impact that is socio-economically beneficial. Her work was exhibited at the Venice Architecture Biennale in 2012 and 2016 and will be exhibited as a solo show at the Louisiana Museum of Modern Art in Humlebaek, Denmark in 2020.
Kundoo is the author of the monograph *Roger Anger: Research on Beauty/ Recherche sur la Beauté, Architecture 1958–2008* (Jovis, Berlin 2009).

| **ANUPAMA KUNDOO**

Installation "The Library of Lost Books" in collaboration with Institute for Advanced Architecture of Catalonia (IAAC), University of Queensland, and TU Berlin under the direction of Anupama Kundoo, Ali Dabirian, Alba Balmaseda, Barcelona 2014

DesignBuild Education and Sociology

ARLENE OAK AND CLAIRE NICHOLAS

DesignBuild education includes settings, activities, and specific circumstances that have a great deal to offer to social scientists. We're most familiar with how DesignBuild can be considered through sociology, so that's what we'll focus on here. There are different definitions of DesignBuild both inside and outside the university context and also across different locations so, just to be clear, when we refer to "DesignBuild" here, we mean those creative projects in higher education that involve students in all stages of the planning and making of a structure (or product) that is intended to be used by people outside the particular, classroom-based design/architecture studio.

A sense of the diversity of DesignBuild education's activities is indicated by the following, from the proceedings document of the 2015 symposium held in Berlin, titled, *DesignBuild-Studio: New Ways in Architectural Education* (edited by architect/educators Ursula Hartig and Nina Pawlicki, who were both at TU Berlin when the document was produced):

"There are [DesignBuild] projects that react to the needs and necessities of 'real' clients whilst others have a more experimental nature. Some are transitory structures, others are meant to last for several decades. Some are co-operations between partner-universities of different countries and cultures, others are country specific."[1]

As is evident by the range of DesignBuild projects mentioned above, this mode of education has something to offer to any sociologist who is interested in finding out about how creativity is performed within and across a range of contexts: from the level of face-to-face dialogue, through community-based engagements, to the concerns of large-scale organizations (such as the Association of Collegiate Schools of Architecture (ACSA) or the European Association for Architectural Education (EAAE)) with what constitutes a "good" education in architecture.

All DesignBuild projects include individuals and groups influencing each other and cooperating across varied activities, from the visualizations required to imagine the future occupants of a building, to the pragmatism required to build within budget; therefore, DesignBuild offers great scope for sociologists who are interested in working with programs of education. By extension, we hope that professors of architecture will consider involving sociologists in some of their projects. The involvement of sociologists with DesignBuild education probably won't help a structure be more beautiful or functional, but it might help designers to be more aware of how creativity happens as a socio-technical process that involves history, community, and negotiation alongside materials, tools, and location.

Cross-disciplinary collaborations between social scientists and architects can help foster understanding between and across academic fields and lead to projects that combine scholarly relevance, pedagogic success, and community-based impact (for an example of such a project, see Verderber, Cavanagh, Oak: *Thinking While Doing: Explorations in*

◀ **Video recordings by researchers on construction site**

Educational Design Build. Basel 2019). This book outlines a series of DesignBuild projects in the USA and Canada that were studied by scholars in the social sciences and humanities. We were involved in this project and found that the interactions between us, as sociologists, and the architecture professors and students we encountered on the specific DesignBuild projects helped foster a better understanding of how scholarship and creative practice interconnect.

In the following discussion, we'll outline a few issues that sociologists often consider, before taking a look at some of the rich areas of research that DesignBuild offers to sociology. We'll finish with a few comments on what DesignBuild education might gain from the engagement of sociologists.

A few words about sociology

Sociology emerged as a scholarly discipline that studied patterns of social relationship through empirical investigation. Given the West's urbanization and industrialization throughout the late 19th and 20th centuries, early sociologists often studied topics such as population mobility, secularization, and social stratification through generating and analyzing "scientific facts" – often presented as statistical information – about the general principles that (seemed to) govern peoples' everyday lives. In contrast, some of the more recent strands of smaller-scale "qualitative" inquiry in sociology often use interviews and/or observations (instead of large-scale questionnaires) to generate insights concerning the values, beliefs, and understandings of the persons being studied.

While sociology has had many influences, a core focus of the discipline has been the relationship in societies between agency and structure. That is, as individuals, do we have the power (i.e. the "agency") to shape our social world, or are the long-standing "structures" of human connection (e.g. religion, politics) so strong that our behaviors and choices are mostly predetermined?

The sociological concern with how agency and structure play out in social groups meant that attention was rarely focused on how individuals or groups engaged with material phenomena – such as tools and technologies – or with physical environments – from clothing to urban developments.

More recently, especially since the latter part of the 20th century, the concern of sociologists with how humans behave in social groups has extended to include an interest in how people create and use technologies, consumer products, and built environments. Often, today, sociologists describe, investigate, and critique the ways in which humans and "non-humans" (i.e. technologies, tools, environments, and infrastructures) interact to create the meanings, communities, and cultures that we live in and through.

DesignBuild's interest to sociology

Whether we consider sociology's traditional focus on agency and/or structure or the discipline's more recent, though connected, engagement with how humans are entwined with materiality, technology, and environments, DesignBuild offers sociologists many interesting topics to explore.

The activities of DesignBuild might be especially relevant for sociologists who seek to understand the institutional and/or interactional levels of society. That is, sociological studies of DesignBuild could consider the politics and economics of how a DesignBuild program fits into a school of architecture (that itself is likely just one component within a larger educational institution); or they could compare different DesignBuild programs or projects to consider, for instance, how projects that orient

Video recordings and notes by sociologists at a DesignBuild meeting

| ARLENE OAK AND CLAIRE NICHOLAS

towards Public Interest Design (where the needs of often-marginalized communities are served by DesignBuild courses) are similar to or different from those projects that emphasize structural, aesthetic, or technological innovation (of course, the same DesignBuild project might cover both orientations).

More "micro-level" sociological studies might consider, for instance, how DesignBuild professors organize students into (more or less) effective teams, how students manage authorship of highly-collaborative projects, or how students and instructors interact with community-based participants to ensure that pedagogic needs are met alongside those of the client. Other micro-level studies might explore how decisions about materials are made, how digital drawings are translated into a three-dimensional model, or how participants manage failure if a project is not successful.

Clearly, the activities of DesignBuild are multifaceted and so offer great scope for sociologists who study how the social world and the techno-material environment are co-created and coexistent. Since DesignBuild education involves the "real" planning and construction of things that will "really" be used, sociologists can study the typical situations through which DesignBuild participants make the decisions that lead to actual buildings. For sociologists who are interested in everyday life, examining the "real" activities of designing and making offers so much more than studying hypothetical situations or researcher-generated experiments: it is in the real instances of practice that the idiosyncrasies of specific projects and the challenges of collaboration are revealed.

Sociology's interest to DesignBuild

We've outlined a few reasons why DesignBuild might be of interest to sociologists, but what about turning the tables – what does sociology offer to the students, educators, or clients of DesignBuild education? Given that many contemporary sociologists consider how humans, materials, tools, and technologies work together, a sociological study that describes how participants translate meaning from, say, rough sketches to models and then to construction drawings, might help designers or builders see where a technical problem or a social miscommunication occurred. DesignBuild activities analyzed through sociological theories might offer perspectives on, for instance, the logistical difficulties of running a DesignBuild program in a traditional academic setting, how DesignBuild might reproduce or challenge architecture education's historic lack of women or persons of color, or how the work of DesignBuild students is perceived by members of a local community.

Students with signed ethics forms

Video recordings of group activities for for the sociologists' research

Arlene Oak is Associate Professor of Material Culture and Design Studies in the Department of Human Ecology at the University of Alberta, Edmonton, Canada. Her background includes undergraduate degrees in studio-based design, an MA in the history of design, and a PhD in the social psychology of design practice. Her research and publications consider how language (especially conversation) relates to the creation and mediation of the material world. Recent projects have focused on architecture education – especially DesignBuild (i.e. "live projects") education – and professional architecture practice. Other recent work explores the presentation and reception of material and visual culture on television and in popular music.

Claire Nicholas is Assistant Professor of Textiles and Material Culture at the University of Nebraska-Lincoln. Her background includes undergraduate studies in design, and an MA and PhD in sociocultural anthropology. Her research and publications focus on the ethnography of craft and design process, pedagogy and the everyday practices (and politics) of making and interpreting material and visual culture. She has conducted fieldwork in Morocco and across North America in contexts ranging from artisanal textile workshops to university architecture studios.

If architecture students, professors, and wider society were to consider DesignBuild projects through a sociological lens, they might find it easier to see the social complexities and implications of this kind of work; its importance as a series of interactions between people, tools, materials, and sites; and its relevance as a kind of informal experiment in the socio-technical phenomena of experiential learning. DesignBuild programs have much to offer to architecture education and to the communities who use and benefit from the projects created, but also to other scholarly disciplines and fields of engaged enquiry.

1   https://issuu.com/cocoon-studio/docs/
cocoon_new_ways_in_arch_education_s.,
p. 18 (accessed 30 November 2019).

The Response-Ability of DesignBuild Programs

DesignBuild projects depend on the "response-ability" of students, on their capacity to understand and manage the many-faceted challenges contained in a project. Some may be more interested in enhancing their portfolio than in how the intervention will affect the community in which the project is be realized. The curse of ArchDaily... It's the "response-ability" of teachers to hold back on these. We should only support projects that hold societal relevance, not merely "cool projects."

Depending on the context, local and well-known or foreign and uncharted, the project should explore and highlight unmet local urban challenges. "Foreign projects" must be grounded in local commitment, i.e. through counterparts, local students, local community organizations or the like, who will take on a personal responsibility once the visiting students leave the site. Because they do. Many — not least the architectural press — seem to forget that banal fact.

DB projects contain two interacting learning dimensions, 1) architecture as a societal act and 2) architecture as an embodied act. The "societal aspect" provides the students with an entrance to the real world. They have to adhere to laws and regulations, to schedules and logistics, to material, machinery, and financial constraints, and crucially, are held personally responsible for their own actions and decisions towards any "third person". Therein lies a critically important difference between studio and DB projects. The "embodied aspect" constitutes the sensory experience of architecture, i.e. of experiencing a line becoming physical. "Only when you have carried stone do you get a sense of how to use stone in your buildings," a colleague once said. As for "design" and "aesthetics," these are end results rather than starting points and beauty seems to emerge out of students working together.

Despite the wide experience from DB projects evidencing the critical professional insights students gain from these programs, not least their understanding of architecture's strategic powers, such programs are still merely add-ons and elective opportunities. Besides Yale, there are only a few schools in the Global South, as far as I know, that have acted on the overwhelming evidence and made DB courses mandatory in preparing the students for the current aggressive professional world.

Hans Skotte is an architect with years of professional experience in Africa and South Asia, aside from public service in Norway. He returned to academia through a PhD and a subsequent professorship focusing among other things on the "power of practice." He ran the Urban Ecological Planning program of the Department of Architecture & Planning at the Norwegian University of Science and Technology (NTNU) in Trondheim, where the introductory semester was spent collaborating with slum dwellers in Kampala, Uganda.

Conflict Urbanization: Visualizing the Political. The Architect as Social Activist

TEDDY CRUZ + FONNA FORMAN

In many ways, DesignBuild physicalizes urgent action in architecture. When it intervenes in sites of marginalization and human hardship, it becomes not only action, but activism in the service of spatial justice. However, we contend that DesignBuild, while attending to the immediacy of crisis, should not be decoupled from a commitment to critical, process-based reflection, becoming a tool to expose the conditions themselves that have produced the crisis. In other words, architects should address themselves not only to "solving" immediate spatial problems, but also to critically investigating and countering the vectors of power that are creating so much social disparity and injustice across the world. Every site of intervention can be seen as a local manifestation of these broader inequalities and injustices; and it is imperative that the architect find mechanisms for orienting herself into the specific site where she wishes to build, constructing her agency through the local voices of those who are struggling against these dynamics of conflict. From its foundation, our research-based political and architecture practice has embedded itself in the Tijuana-San Diego border region, pushing ahead as a global laboratory for engaging the central challenges of urbanization today: deepening social and economic inequality, dramatic migratory shifts, urban informality, climate change, the thickening of border walls, and the decline of public thinking. And now that Tijuana and San Diego have become the main site of arrival for people seeking asylum from Central American violence and poverty, geopolitics has once more turned intensely local.

This urges us to localize the global, moving from a critical distance, the abstraction of globalization (the "out there" somewhere in the world), into the specificity of the political inscribed in the physical territory, a critical proximity (the "here and now" of our immediate political context). This also means moving simultaneously across scales, from the global border to the border region, to the border neighborhood, in order to understand the implications of global conflict in shaping the contested power relations inscribed in the everyday lives of people impacted by those conflicts on the political ground itself.

◄◄
The stairs and pier at the end of Kongens Gata in Kjøpmannsgata, Trondheim are a project by Anders Gunleiksrud and John Haddal Mork of NTNU Live Studio, 2014

◄
The 5 Ws, Estudio Teddy Cruz + Fonna Forman, 2014

The Tijuana–San Diego
border region:
a geography of conflict

| TEDDY CRUZ + FONNA FORMAN

In our practice, architecture is not only, or primarily, about spatial-material intervention, but about constructing methods for visualizing political and civic processes, the urban conflicts and controversies that result from the collision between top-down policies of exclusionary urbanization and bottom-up social and ecological networks. How can we tackle the urban crisis without visualizing it, without "naming" the forces that produced it? In other words, the critical knowledge of the conditions that produced the global crisis should be the material for architects in our time, making urban conflict the most important creative tool to reimagine the city today.

For us, Conflict Urbanization is the process of naming and operationalizing precise global, regional, and urban borders where discriminatory and alienating policies – by design – exert specific pressure, colliding with spatial, social, and environmental conditions. This means shifting our gaze from the privileged sites of development to the peripheral zones of crisis. It demands a new praxis of intervention, engaging the conditions themselves that have produced such collision, as the material for design.

Recognizing urban conflict as a point of departure and as an operational tool requires expanded modes of practice, through which architects can be responsible for imagining counter-spatial procedures; political and economic structures that can produce new modes of sociability and encounter. We maintain that exposing and altering the exclusionary policies that have produced the current crises should in fact be the first act in the production of a more experimental architecture, which can only emerge from engaging with and negotiating today's conflict urbanizations as the radical context from which to produce new programmatic, formal, and aesthetic categories that problematize the relationship between the social, the institutional, and the spatial.

Our projects always begin with a *Conflict Diagram*, a method to name and visualize a particular urban conflict, including a relational cartography of the multiple conditions inscribed in a contested site, the political, social, and economic power relations embedded within it, as well as the diverse stakeholders, top-down and bottom-up, involved in the conflict – those who have produced the crisis, those affected by it, and those activist practices that are mobilized to tackle the crisis. The Conflict Diagram is a generative tool for proposition, which is rooted in the controversies, contingencies, and opportunities of a given site or condition. It is a script for intervention, organized around direct questions and provocations that we refer to as the 5 Ws: the where, why, what, who and when of the problem, and its opportunities.

Ultimately, the Conflict Diagram becomes a how, an anticipatory framework that sets up the terms for intervention. In other words, conflict diagrams not only expose the complex vectors of force embedded in any crisis, but also set up the designing of conditions within which "things can happen".

In our work, visualizing the political is the prerequisite for a more effective and inclusive urban and architectural DesignBuild. For us, this is a double project of research and action, which begins with positioning ourselves dialectically within the specificity of urban conflicts, exposing hidden institutional histories in order to piece together a more accurate anticipatory urban research and design intervention. This requires taking the necessary detours to contact the many domains and their procedural intelligence that have remained peripheral to design. For us, then, the visualization of the political does not stop at the naming or measuring of the problem, but also involves producing research and design strategies to transcend it. We are designing not only physical things, but also the programmatic framework to reorganize institutional protocols, knowledge, and resources; to increase community capacities for political action.

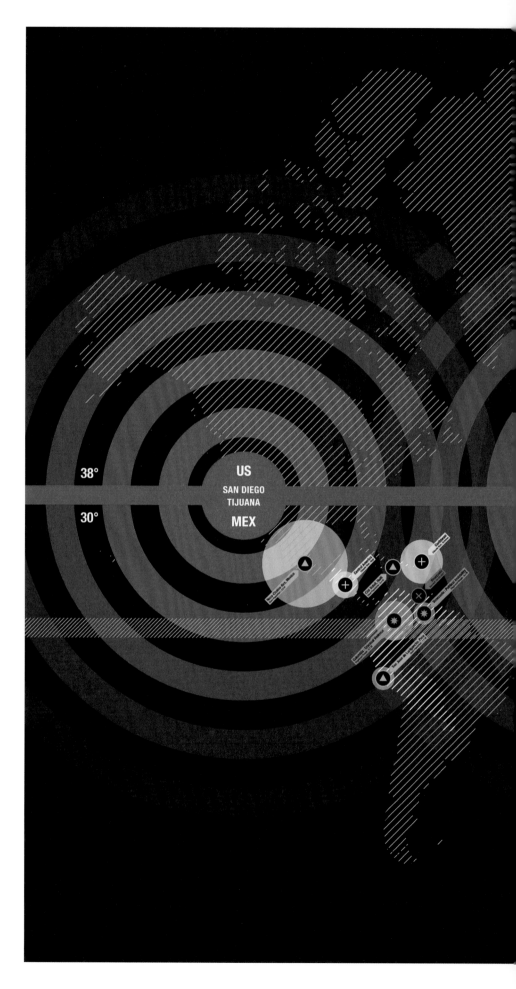

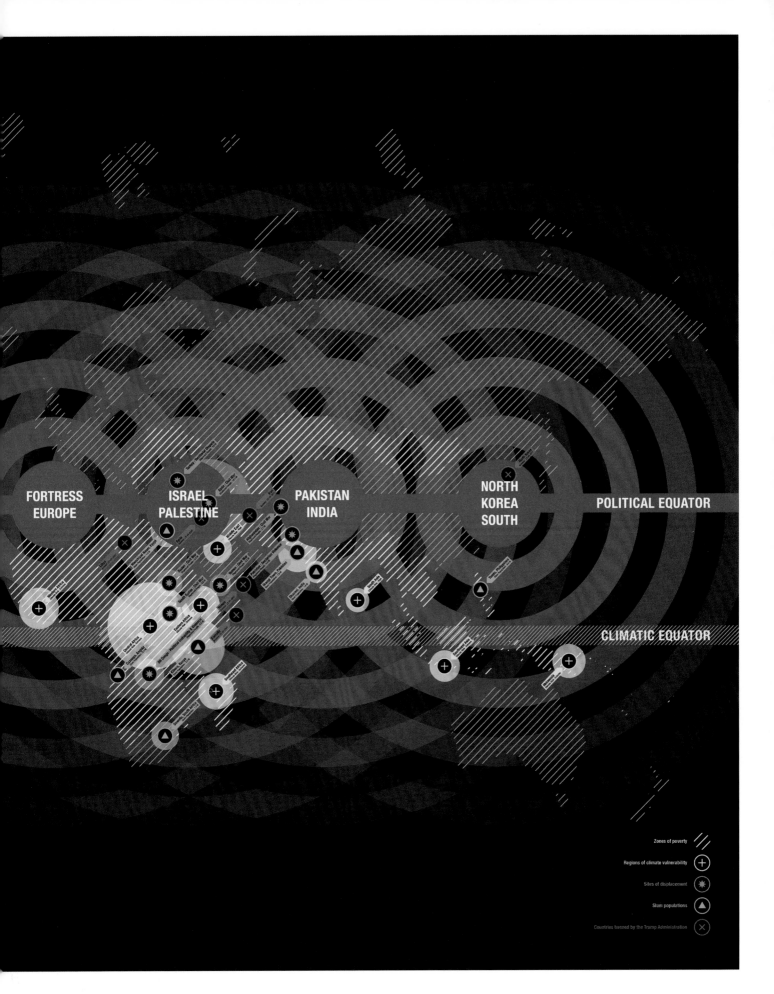

FORTRESS
EUROPE

ISRAEL
PALESTINE

PAKISTAN
INDIA

NORTH
KOREA
SOUTH

POLITICAL EQUATOR

CLIMATIC EQUATOR

Zones of poverty

Regions of climate vulnerability

Sites of displacement

Slum populations

Countries banned by the Trump Administration

Architect as social activist: designing urban rights

Our practice is an unconventional partnership between a political theorist and an architect. We investigate "informal" urban dynamics and emergent collective practices – social, moral, economic, political, spatial. We are particularly interested in how people in conditions of scarcity, on the margins of formal institutions, build informal settlements, markets of exchange, governance practices and general strategies of collective survival. Our research has always been motivated by the positive impact of immigrants on the city. Their ingenious strategies of adaptation and survival in conditions of scarcity have inspired our urban vision. For us, border neighborhoods are sites of urban and political creativity that can generate more inclusive imaginaries of urban development.

The border neighborhoods we engage in our work are sites of amazing informal resilience and creativity. But this ingenuity is typically off the radar of formal institutions with power and resources – hidden behind an undifferentiated screen of poverty and criminality and all the biases people associate with these conditions. We believe these informal practices need documentation and translation. Informal settlements across the world are stealthily shaping a new politics of urban growth for the contemporary city, largely unobserved by those who formally define the categories of urban development. The "official city" can learn from these urban processes. Peripheral communities are not passive victims of poverty. They are intensely active urban agents who are capable of challenging the dominant models of growth that have excluded them, and denied their rights to the city. This creative knowledge needs to trickle up, to inspire policymakers and planners to rethink their approaches to the city.

We have come to see urban rights less as a set of mandates designed from above (the conventional way of thinking about rights), and more as a set of performative urban actions from below. This bottom-up action can take the shape of emergent, everyday, lived practices among marginalized communities, or more deliberate strategies of urban intervention designed to counter exclusionary political and economic power. We have argued that these bottom-up social and economic exchanges, spatial flows, and actions are the building blocks for a more just and equitable city. Contrasting the neoliberal hegemony that organizes the global city through logics of consumption, privatization, and display, these informal urbanizations at the margins sustain themselves with their own resources through logics of local productivity, negotiating time, space, boundaries, and resources in conditions of scarcity and emergency. In these peripheral communities we find economic configurations emerging and thriving through tactical adaptation and retrofit that transgress discriminatory zoning and exclusionary economic development.

Urban rights should be understood as a collective practice of resistance to unjust power structures in the city – the urban norms, policies, procedures, and spaces that perpetuate uneven patterns of urban development. Urban activism should focus on increasing public knowledge, rejecting hierarchical social norms that validate neglect, exploitation and dispossession in the city, igniting civic dignity, repairing public trust, and restoring a belief in community agency at the local scale. In this sense, we very much see ourselves as curators of knowledge, urban translators, and facilitators of bottom-up intelligence to cultivate new communities of practice. Every project we do is a process of curating participation across sectors, convening the knowledges and resources that are necessary to conceive, design, fund, permit, build, and program an intervention and sustain it in the long term. Design-Build for us means not only building inclusive spaces, but advancing urban rights, and participating in the co-production of the city.

| TEDDY CRUZ + FONNA FORMAN

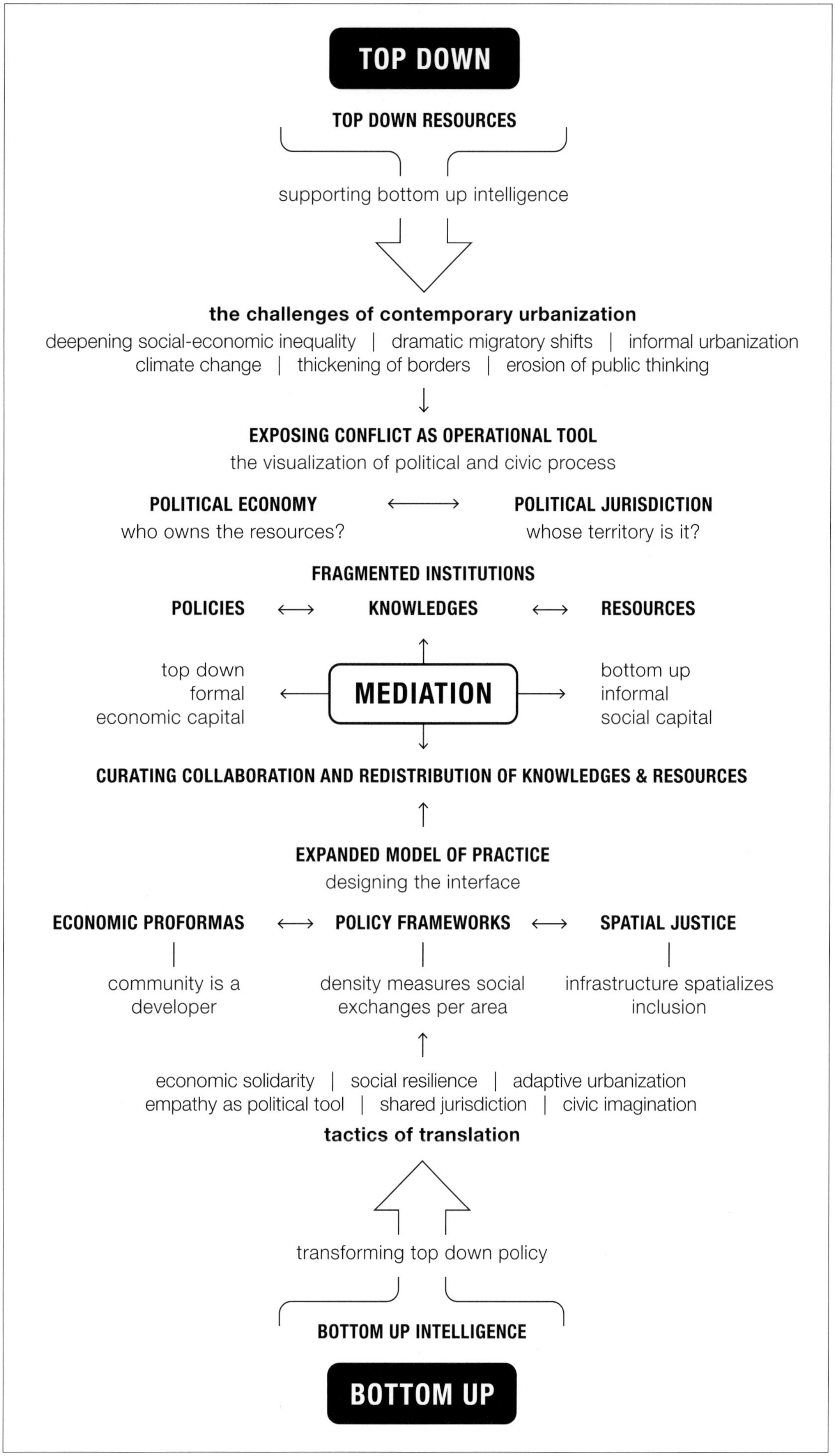

TOP DOWN

TOP DOWN RESOURCES

supporting bottom up intelligence

the challenges of contemporary urbanization

deepening social-economic inequality | dramatic migratory shifts | informal urbanization
climate change | thickening of borders | erosion of public thinking

↓

EXPOSING CONFLICT AS OPERATIONAL TOOL

the visualization of political and civic process

POLITICAL ECONOMY ⟷ **POLITICAL JURISDICTION**

who owns the resources?   whose territory is it?

FRAGMENTED INSTITUTIONS

POLICIES ⟷ **KNOWLEDGES** ⟷ **RESOURCES**

top down   bottom up
formal   ← **MEDIATION** →   informal
economic capital   social capital

CURATING COLLABORATION AND REDISTRIBUTION OF KNOWLEDGES & RESOURCES

↑

EXPANDED MODEL OF PRACTICE

designing the interface

ECONOMIC PROFORMAS ⟷ **POLICY FRAMEWORKS** ⟷ **SPATIAL JUSTICE**

community is a   density measures social   infrastructure spatializes
developer   exchanges per area   inclusion

↑

economic solidarity | social resilience | adaptive urbanization
empathy as political tool | shared jurisdiction | civic imagination

tactics of translation

transforming top down policy

BOTTOM UP INTELLIGENCE

BOTTOM UP

Conflict Diagram, 2014

Teddy Cruz + Fonna Forman are
principals in *Estudio Teddy Cruz +
Fonna Forman,* a research-based political and architectural practice in San
Diego investigating issues of informal
urbanization, civic infrastructure, and
public culture. Transcending conventional boundaries between theory and
practice, and the fields of architecture
and urbanism, political theory, and
urban policy, Cruz + Forman lead a variety of urban research agendas in the
San Diego-Tijuana border region and
beyond. From 2012 to 2013 they served
as special advisors on civic and urban
initiatives for the City of San Diego
and led the development of its Civic
Innovation Lab. Together they lead the
UCSD Community Stations, a platform
for community-engaged research and
teaching on poverty and social equity
in the border region. Their work has
been exhibited widely in prestigious cultural venues across the world, including MoMA in New York, YBCA in San
Francisco, the Cooper Hewitt National
Design Museum in New York, and the US
Pavilion at the 2018 Venice Architecture
Biennale. **Teddy Cruz** is a professor
of Public Culture and Urbanism in the
Department of Visual Arts at UC San
Diego. **Fonna Forman** is a professor
of Political Theory and the founding
director of the Center on Global Justice
at UC San Diego.

P. Mecalux Retrofit.
Factory-adapted parts
for self-made housing.
Estudio Teddy Cruz +
Fonna Forman, 2015

Learning as Architects to Affect Social Impact Through Collaboration on the DesignBuild Site

Our education program began as a response to the challenges a group of us were facing as architects as we tried to address the difficult challenges faced by our client communities. As a group of young architects coming into practice from the so-called developing world, our concern was for those left behind, marginalized, and excluded who were often our clients. Could design be a more inclusionary act and serve clients and needs that we were not trained to engage with in our education as architects? So many of the methods, practices, and models we were taught in our training left us ill-equipped to deal with the realities and needs of so much of the world we practiced in. So we embarked on a search to expand these skills and practices as professionals, and then educators. As educators, this concern became an impetus for rethinking the pedagogy of architecture – how to effectively teach the skills, protocols, and methods we were finding were needed to engage with the problems we were facing in the field. In the early 1980s, the then-emerging model of DesignBuild education seemed to offer us a pedagogical framework for our rethinking of the architecture curriculum. Our curriculum evolved to frame the DesignBuild process, and the construction site itself, as a site of learning. Constructed as a site, and as a process of learning by doing, the construction site became for us, as educators, the necessary "real world" context where students and clients exchange and learn from each other. The collaboration and exchange of knowledge makes possible the successful completion of projects within the context of limited resources and marginalisation that most of our clients live in. Framed as such, the architecture project becomes a co-production co-production by the client/community it serves and the students, who are learning to be citizens as they learn the practice of architecture.

Sergio Palleroni is an architect and professor as well as Director of the Center for Public Interest Design (CPID), a research institute founded at Portland State University in 2013. He was previously a professor at the University of Texas, Austin, and at the University of Washington for two decades, where he founded the Basic Initiative, a multidisciplinary fieldwork program which each year challenges students from the USA and abroad to apply their education in service of the problems facing marginalized communities throughout the world.

Built Degree

JUAN ROMÁN

The "Pabellón Restos Frente al Horizonte" (Pavilion Fragment Facing the Horizon) on Curanipe Beach is the work realized by Felipe Muñoz in 2012 that allowed him to graduate from the School of Architecture at the University of Talca in Chile. In doing so, Felipe completed the six years of studies evoke an architectural training in Chile. The structure's form aims to recreate the image of the disaster that we Chileans faced when waking up on 27 February 2010, after the earthquake and the tsunami that had hit the country before dawn. In that sense, Felipe's work is both protective pavilion and a memorial to the tragedy, or to the image of the tragedy. It stands on two rocks protruding from the sand level of the beach, with a space between them in which people find shelter from the coastal wind. Composed of two large trusses placed perpendicular to the horizon, it is tied together by an ordered disorder of wooden planks, some of which were gathered by Felipe just a couple of days after 27 February 2010, when the earth was still trembling. I have seen the way the sand level changes in time, the way it moves up and down following the tidal waves. The rocks sometimes stand four meters tall and sometimes barely half a meter is visible. The work is constantly changing, not only due to the visual vibration in the apparent chaos of the planks with which it was built, but also because it suggests different ways for the place to be inhabited in time.

The following paragraphs introduce the ideas that explain the process behind the work of Felipe Muñoz. Those ideas led a small school of a small city in a small country to decide back in the year 2004 that a built work would be the means to obtain the architecture degree in the sixth year of studies. It is a process that involves conceiving of, designing, resource-raising for, building, and reporting on a work that is guided by the following considerations:

- Architectural education institutions have two responsibilities: first, to ensure graduates are capable of playing the role society expects of them, i.e. of designing buildings able to last for a sustainable period of time. Second, to prepare those graduates to be able to perform appropriately in an adequately paid job.
- Labor market changes have been rapid enough for us to observe how futile the effort can be that architecture school students and professors dedicate to the teaching-learning process of building design every year as the only skill that is exclusive to the architectural profession.
- The enormous effort of the traditional graduation track, whose final product is a set of plans and models, lives and dies within academia. Remarkably, it is thanks to this academic work that universities grant a professional degree allowing the graduates to operate in society, without any prior practical experience. This does not seem very prudent.

◀◀
The pavilion of the Druk White Lotus School in Ladakh, Himalaya, India, was a project of the Center for Public Interest Design, 2010

◀
Final project by María Jesús Molina, School of Architecture, University of Talca, Chile

- A traditional graduation project in Chile demands that a student spend approximately US$2,000 because it necessitates hiring others to help in the making of drawings, renderings, and models in order to be able to deliver the project in due time according to the university schedule. Spending such an amount of money on the making of products that are likely to be forgotten somewhere in a corner soon does not seem particularly worthwhile. All the more, when in an economically underdeveloped country like Chile, US$2,000 are enough to build, let's say, 10 square meters of a building, somewhere.
- A graduation project, whatever its track, should allow to verify that every competency declared in the study plan of the school of architecture granting the degree has been effectively taught to every student. In this way the built work, however small it may be, is steeped in reality and therefore establishes a complex problem that sufficiently verifies whether the student is proficient enough to be granted an architect's professional degree.

In the above-mentioned way, 500 works were built between 2004 and 2019 in the territories associated with the Central Valley in Chile, where the school is located. A process that informs the following afterthoughts 15 years later:

- The built works could be understood as a contribution to a discussion on the ties that can be established between university and society. However, in this case the reverse process is far more interesting: the ties that can be established between society and university. The students of the School of Architecture of Talca, like many other inhabitants of the Central Valley in Chile, have strong ties with the land economically and culturally way, and these ties may

Pabellón Restos Frente al Horizonte (Pavilion Fragment Facing the Horizon). Final project by Felipe Muñoz, School of Architecture, University of Talca, Chile

resonate in their built works. Therefore the School of Architecture contributes to creating space within the university in ways peculiar to those who inhabit the region.

- Universities from developed countries invest resources in technology that is able to simulate reality inside academia. Since those resources are not available in Talca, students leave the world of academia behind to delve into reality.
- The circumstances of developing the graduation works both inside and outside determine a space full of dichotomies. These include carefulness and risk, thinking and acting, but also the eagerness demanded by tutors and the banalization of the works stemming from a conformist view of both workers and neighbors, who are habituated to things being as usual and not as they could be. Nevertheless, by the end of the building process, those dichotomies are present as a space in which they coexist as non-exclusionary dualities.
- There is an added value in this: after completing their works, the graduated students already have a small network consisting of workers, neighbors, managers, and businessmen. These are the ones their works have reached, and the ones that will allow the graduates to approach their first jobs as architects. This is something.
- The precondition that students must raise the building funds themselves almost immediately gives their projects a public interest, since nobody will invest in a project that is not needed. On the other hand, as money is always scarce, the projects achieve precision in the way they are resolved thanks to a very efficient way of dealing with resources involved in the process: site features, neighbors' consent, availability of materials...

Final project by Diego Orellana, School of Architecture, University of Talca, Chile

Juan Román was born in Chile in 1955. He has a degree in architecture from the University of Valparaiso (1983), a Master in Urban Development from Polytechnic University of Catalonia (2005), and a PhD in Architecture and Heritage from University of Seville (2015). In 1998 he was given the task of developing the project to create the School of Architecture of the University of Talca, where he is currently Head Professor and Dean of the Faculty of Architecture, Music, and Design. His contribution to architectural education in Chile has been recognized in a series of monographies published in Chile and abroad, including *Talca, Cuestión de Educación* (Editorial Arquine, Mexico 2013), *Talca Inédito* (Editorial Pequeño Dios, Chile 2013) and *Inhabiting the Territory* (Quodlibet Studio, Italy 2015). In 2015 he was given the Global Award for Sustainable Architecture by the Locus Foundation in Paris, France. In 2016 he was the curator of the Chilean pavilion for the 15th Venice Biennale.

For many years the School of Talca had addressed the final project with an oscillating approach, proceeding from territory to detail and from detail to territory. However, since the first project was built in 2004, it now appears to be based on an approach that proceeds almost exclusively from detail to territory. It gives an account of the students' capacity to include the whole in a small part. Comparing the architecture conceived in an approach from detail to territory and the models for bottom-up development demonstrates that operating simultaneously on both the local and the global aspects of a territory is a method that is particular to the Architecture School of Talca.

◄
Final project by Javiera
Navarro, School of
Architecture, University
of Talca, Chile

Globe with projects by
Benny Nast

Sunderpur Housing

BIHAR, INDIA **BASEHABITAT, UNIVERSITY OF ART AND DESIGN LINZ**

Function: Residential building, open areas
Size: 400 m² per building
Building material: Loam bricks (adobe), bricks, concrete, steel, bamboo

Research phase: 10.2015
Planning phase: 10.2015–01.2016
Building phase: 01.2016–07.2017, **(1st phase:** 01.2016–02.2016, **2nd phase:** 09.2016–12.2016, **3rd phase:** 02.2017–07.2017)

Students: 30
Further participants on construction site: 18
Lecturers: 2

Client: Little Flower Leprosy Welfare Association
Cost: approx. EUR 90,000
Financed by: State of Upper Austria, Karl Zünd Foundation, Pancivis Foundation, Little Flower Leprosy Welfare Association, private donors

Project initiated by: BASEhabitat; Little Flower Leprosy Welfare Association
Project led by: Dominik Abbrederis, Ulrike Schwantner, Wolfgang Fiel (BASEhabitat)

1 | Public space between the buildings

2 | Drying loam bricks (adobe) for construction of the residential buildings

3 | Trial application of various plasters

4 | Furnished bedroom in one of the residential buildings

As a studio within the University of Art and Design Linz, BASEhabitat offers a Master of Architecture and a postgraduate Master of Advanced Studies – Architecture. The studio has been active internationally in the area of sustainable, socially responsible architecture for many years and has been able to realize mainly residential houses, kindergartens, and schools for the socially disadvantaged on several continents.

The housing project is based on a master plan for Sunderpur and the Phoolna Development project completed here earlier, as part of which BASEhabitat built new apartments for teachers between 2012 and 2015. Sunderpur is a former leper colony in the Indian State of Bihar on the border with Nepal. Several generations of patients still live there today, and a large number of Indian leprosy patients are treated every year. Since 1981, a hospital, a school, a dairy, and a weaving mill have been built here by the Indian organization Little Flower Leprosy Welfare Association founded by Brother Christdas. The aim of the village's further development is not only to treat and support patient recovery, but also to fight the stigma associated with the disease, as well as to create workplaces to help affected persons out of their poverty.

The construction of the new two-story buildings was prepared by a group of students during a two-week research trip in October 2015. Talks with the inhabitants of the settlement took place after a review of the situation, detailed surveying of the existing buildings, and an update of the available plans. This was intended to help the students to gain a better

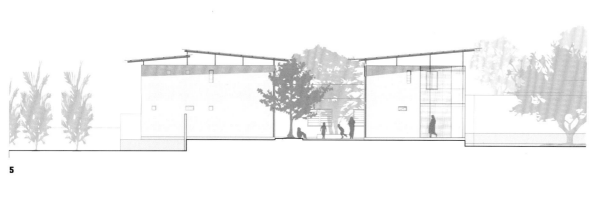

5

7

6

understanding of the population's living conditions: How many people live together in one room? How are the rooms arranged? Where do people meet? Knowledge about the way people live, local habits, and lifestyle was intended to significantly influence the later design. The BASEhabitat students used this information to create detailed maps while analyzing the living situation of each family of the community of 800 people. The design aimed to use local construction materials to build 12 sample apartments with a flexible internal layout, which were also intended to serve as a starting point for future independent housing projects. In order to improve the sanitary situation, the new construction was to be equipped with one of the first indoor toilets and a direct water supply to the apartments. Earthquake resistance was another important criterion for the design, while the new residential buildings were also required to reflect the change in generations. Offspring of former lepers still live in Sunderpur today, even though they do not have the disease.

The buildings were planned at the University of Art and Design Linz together with experts from the University of Natural Resources and Life Sciences Vienna and TU Vienna, and built by local construction workers and students of the University of Art and Design Linz. An important aspect was the exchange of knowledge between locals, students, and planners on the building site regarding handling local materials such as loam bricks, straw, and bamboo as well as the realization of plans using local building methods and tools.

Two rows of buildings forming a common inner courtyard were erected. Generously projecting roofs protect from rain and heat. The orientation of the houses to the yard shields from the bustle of the village, while also creating a common space for the residents. Verandas and terraces permit visual contact and allow people to meet, offering a semi-public space together with the entrance areas and the stairs. Residents can retreat to their living quarters for privacy. The two building rows differ in terms of the residential units' depth and size. Three-room apartments over two stories are accommodated in the eastern row. These are intended for families in which several generations live together. The kitchen, toilet, and laundry facilities on the ground floor are shared. Smaller, single-story units with their own sanitary and cooking areas are located in the western row of buildings. It was, however, not possible to fit every building with a water connection.

TF

5 | South elevation of housing complex

6| Section of housing complex

7 | Loam brick walls

8 | Water in Sunderpur, from the research paper "Sanitary Facilities in Sunderpur" by Flavia Matei and Max Weidacher

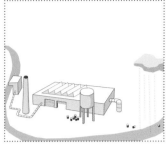

WATER POLLUTION
The water of the river is very polluted. According to the villagers, factories direct their wastewater into the river. The groundwater is likely to be contaminated.

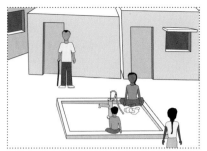

WELLS
Wells act as community hubs in many parts of the village and are also used for personal hygiene. The downside is a lack of privacy regarding personal hygiene.

WASTEWATER
The village women usually wash the dishes directly in front of their houses. The functionality of the open canals should be checked.

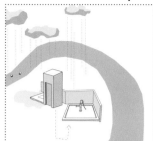

CESSPITS
Many of the wells are situated questionably close to the cesspits of the toilet facilities. It is imperative that water samples are taken.

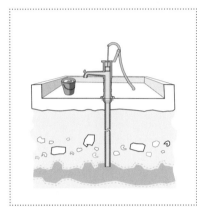

GROUNDWATER WELL

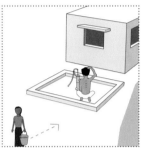

PERSONAL HYGIENE OF MEN
The village men enjoy the privilege of being able to wash themselves at any time of day directly at the public wells, wearing undergarments.

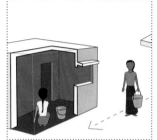

PERSONAL HYGIENE OF WOMEN
Personal hygiene in public is strictly prohibited for women. They go to their houses for personal hygiene and wash themselves under their clothes.

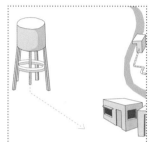

WATER TOWER
The organization Little Flower has started the construction of a water tower. The tower is intended to supply every household with water.

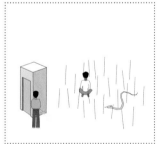

OVERCROWDING
On average, three families share one toilet. This extreme overcrowding leads to long waiting times. The toilets turn into areas of conflict.

CONSEQUENCE
As a direct consequence of the lack of toilets, the areas around the sanitary facilities are frequently soiled with feces.

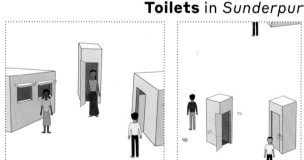
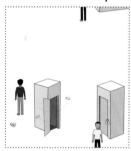

PRIVACY
Women report a lack of privacy due to the exposed location of the toilets. Consequently, women use the toilets as rarely as possible.

LOCKS
Most of the toilets are fitted with locks. Unlocked toilets are usually soiled.

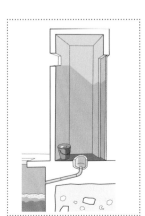

SECTION OF TOILET

PLACES OF FEAR
Due to the lack of lighting, the toilet facilities turn into places of fear, particularly at night. Women avoid using the toilets after nightfall.

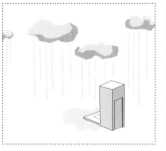

CESSPITS
The villagers complain about all the cesspits overflowing during the rainy season. Nobody could remember the cesspits ever having been emptied.

BIOGAS PLANTS
The village produces biogas from cow dung using a biogas plant. Human feces could also be outgassed in the digestion towers and subsequently composted.

9

Dwelling in Sunderpur,
2015

Well *per Block*

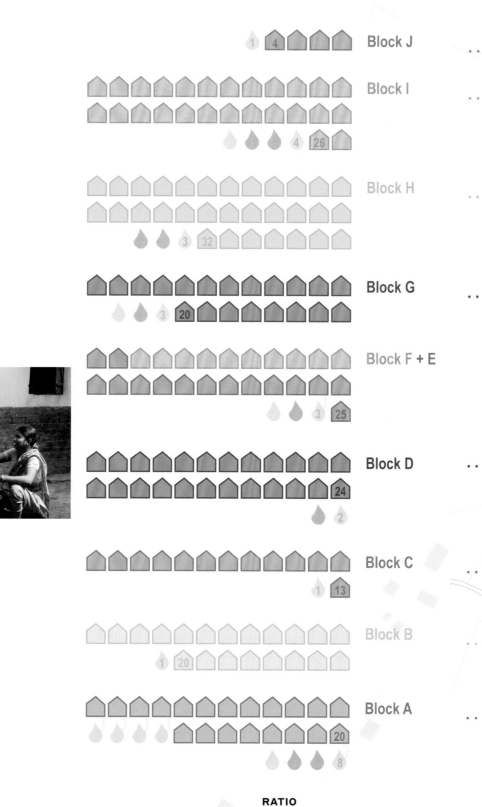

Block J   1 · 4

Block I   4 · 26

Block H   3 · 32

Block G   3 · 20

Block F + E   3 · 25

Block D   24 · 2

Block C   1 · 13

Block B   1 · 20

Block A   20 · 8

10 | Village life with well
in Sunderpur

11 | Well per block, from
the research paper
"Sanitary Facilities
in Sunderpur" by
Flavia Matei and Max
Weidacher

RATIO
wells/households

26   **SUNDERPUR**
184

11

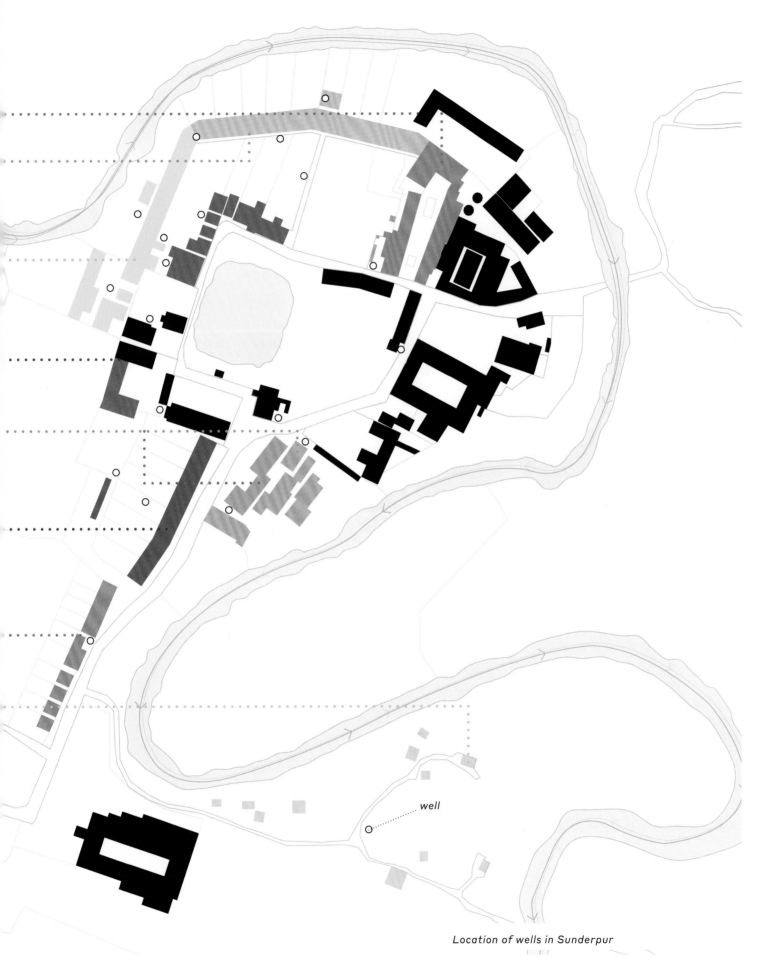

Location of wells in Sunderpur

Toilets *in Sunderpur*

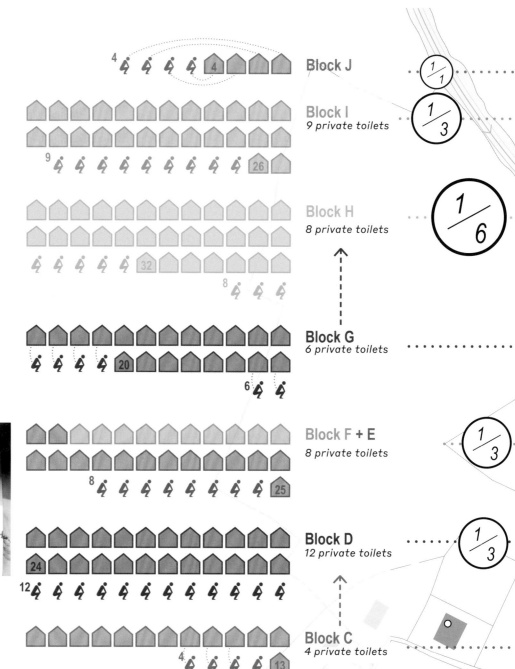

Block J

Block I
9 private toilets

Block H
8 private toilets

Block G
6 private toilets

Block F + E
8 private toilets

Block D
12 private toilets

Block C
4 private toilets

Block B

Block A
1 private toilet

12 | Inspection of the existing sanitary facilities

13 | Toilets in Sunderpur, from the research paper "Sanitary Facilities in Sunderpur" by Flavia Matei and Max Weidacher

13

RATIO
toilets / households   lack of toilets   toilets   households

 132 + **52** = 184

SUNDERPUR

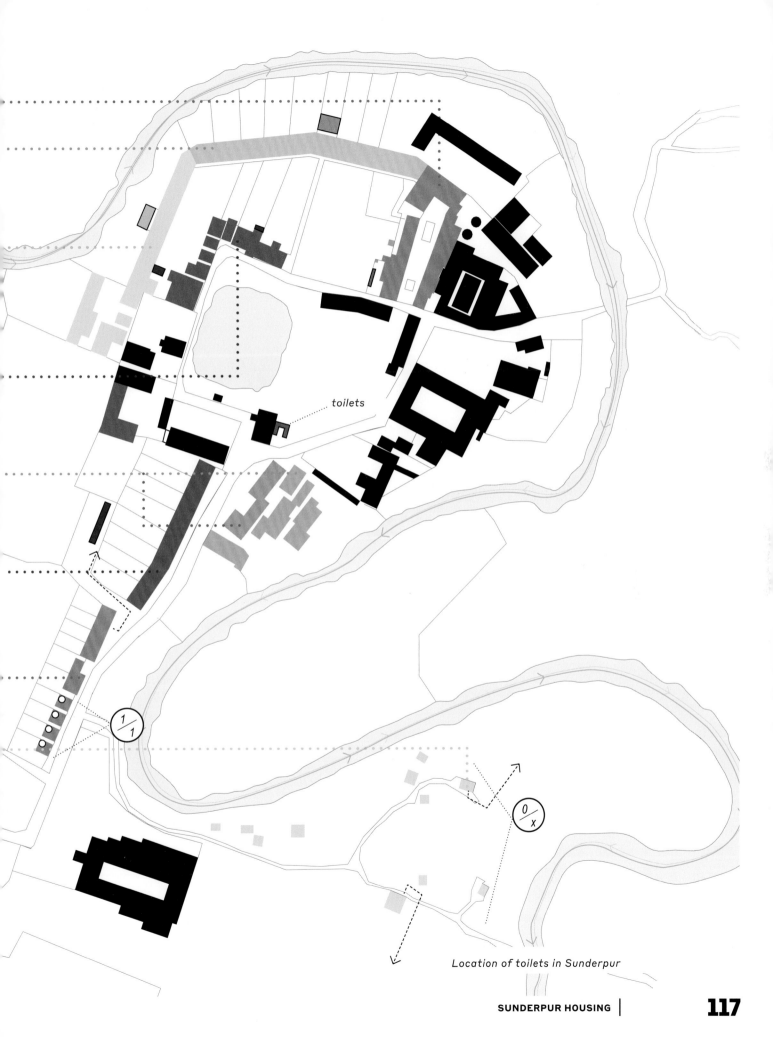

toilets

1/1

0/x

Location of toilets in Sunderpur

Co-Housing Oldenburg / Home not Shelter!

OLDENBURG, GERMANY

TECHNICAL UNIVERSITY OF BERLIN;
JADE UNIVERSITY OF APPLIED SCIENCES OLDENBURG

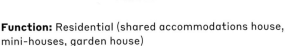

Function: Residential (shared accommodations house, mini-houses, garden house)
Size: 450 m²
Building material: Wood (timber frame construction)

Research phase: 04.2017–03.2018
Planning phase: 04.2018–07.2019
Building phase: 01.2020–12.2020 (estimated)

Students: 11
Lecturers: 4

Client: GSG Oldenburg Bau- und Wohngesellschaft
Expected cost: EUR 1,022,000
Financed by: GSG Oldenburg Bau- und Wohngesellschaft

Project initiated by: Home not Shelter! initiative,
Ralf Pasel (TU Berlin), Hans Drexler (Jade University of Applied Sciences, Oldenburg); Ralph Boch (Hans Sauer Stiftung, Munich)
Project led by: Ralf Pasel (TU Berlin) with Katharina Neubauer and Marie Deilmann

1 | Model of final design

2 | Visualization of attic room interior

3 | Visualization of garden house to be built from the garages

4 | Visualization of housing complex

This experimental housing project focusing on the need for integrative and affordable urban living space was designed within the scope of the Home not Shelter! initiative. A working group composed of the City of Oldenburg, GSG Oldenburg Bau- und Wohngesellschaft, Hans Sauer Foundation, Jade UAS Oldenburg, and TU Berlin was formed for the pilot project to be realized in Oldenburg. The project aims to create a co-housing community of students, families and single parents, refugees, senior citizens, and people with disabilities on a total area of 275 m². The initiative Home not Shelter! specifies that projects must be realized in a participative and collaborative process. Future residents should therefore also be involved in the realization of the construction, following the design process within the scope of a DesignBuild approach.

Vertical studios with lecturers and students in different years of academic study were used to restructure the traditional planning process. The selection of the plot and the conception of the spatial program were preceded by a phase involving an analysis of the thematic context and the determined design, spatial, and programmatic requirements. This was possible because the project was not governed by a specific architectural contract, but carried out as a research project by the initiative Home not Shelter!, which concerns itself with the question of transitory forms of living. What housing requirements do people new to the city have? What do their everyday lives have in common? These can be students, refugees, but also

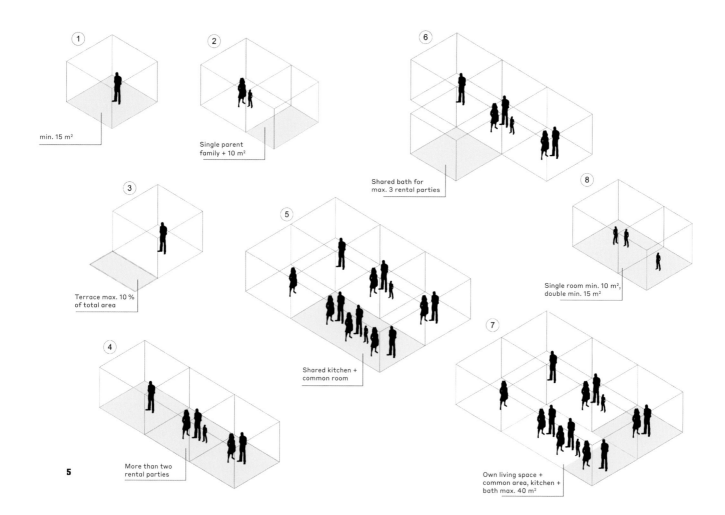

① min. 15 m²

② Single parent family + 10 m²

③ Terrace max. 10 % of total area

④ More than two rental parties

⑤ Shared kitchen + common room

⑥ Shared bath for max. 3 rental parties

⑦ Own living space + common area, kitchen + bath max. 40 m²

⑧ Single room min. 10 m², double min. 15 m²

5

professionals or artists, and they form a new group of city dwellers that generally have something in common with regard to time: they usually do not know how long they will stay.

Under the guidance of Ralf Pasel and his team, students at TU Berlin spent several semesters identifying topics that would become central in the design of such housing typologies: minimal and flexible housing structures, participation in the design of living space (co-designing), identification with a place, as well as minimal private living spaces in favor of generous common areas (co-living). Design phases were accompanied by case studies of micro-apartments and site analyses of potential plots. Since the architecture was to involve a prefabricated timber frame system, seminars on timber construction were also conducted and a variety of models on different scales produced. Based on this, the studio developed an additive ground plan system for the apartments, allowing calculation of a specific number of square meters of private and shared space, depending on the people concerned, which in turn influences the configuration. Overall, the research project can be regarded as mutually influenced between location-specific conditions and the complex task assignment.

In the meantime, under the guidance of Hans Drexler, students at Jade University of Applied Sciences

Oldenburg developed a housing typology referred to as "Mini-Hundehütte". This was inspired by the design of a traditional housing type with a simple gabled roof, common in Oldenburg between about 1875 and 1920 and referred to as "Hundehütte" (dog shed). The structure was split and rearranged as an ensemble in the form of four mini-houses, with the shed roofs facing towards the course of the sun. The final design includes three such mini-houses containing four residential units, occupying a footprint of only 35 m². Located opposite is a large, commonly used residential house accommodating co-living functions for all the residents, such as cooking, washing, playing, and working, and offering spaces for integrative shared living. The scope of the DesignBuild seminar also includes the conversion of garages on the plot into a communal building by the students a well as the future residents. Apart from forming the new central area on the grounds, the garages are also a communal building project that will sustainably promote cohesion of the new residential community. In future, residents will also take charge of designing the garden, a greenhouse, and the interior finishing.

SBA

6   **East view**

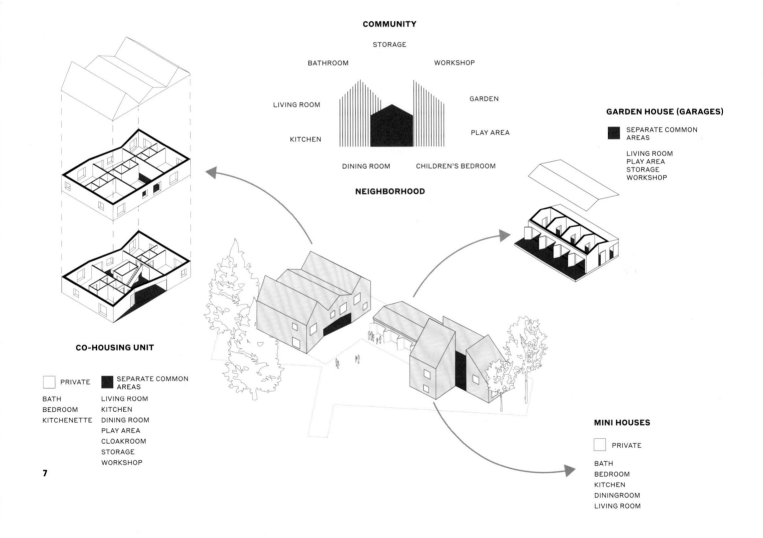

COMMUNITY

STORAGE

BATHROOM   WORKSHOP

LIVING ROOM   GARDEN

KITCHEN   PLAY AREA

DINING ROOM   CHILDREN'S BEDROOM

NEIGHBORHOOD

GARDEN HOUSE (GARAGES)

■ SEPARATE COMMON
   AREAS

LIVING ROOM
PLAY AREA
STORAGE
WORKSHOP

CO-HOUSING UNIT

☐ PRIVATE   ■ SEPARATE COMMON
                      AREAS

BATH   LIVING ROOM
BEDROOM   KITCHEN
KITCHENETTE   DINING ROOM
                  PLAY AREA
                  CLOAKROOM
                  STORAGE
                  WORKSHOP

7

MINI HOUSES

☐ PRIVATE

BATH
BEDROOM
KITCHEN
DININGROOM
LIVING ROOM

5 | **Study on space
requirement**

6 | **East elevation of
housing complex**

7 | **Conceptual represen-
tation of room layout**

1
2

Centro Comunal Alto Perú

CHORRILLOS, LIMA, PERU

E1NSZUE1NS, UNIVERSITY OF STUTTGART

3

Function: Community center with child daycare facility, library, workshop, communal kitchen, dining room
Size: 145 m²
Building material: Regional, handmade loam bricks (adobe), local timbers, load-bearing components made of reinforced steel

Research phase: 09.04.2018–05.05.2018
Planning phase: 06.05.2018–19.07.2018
Building phase: not realized

Students: 12 (University of Stuttgart), 7 (Peruvian students)
Lecturers: 9

Client: Alto Perú Neighborhood

Project initiated by: Hannah Klug (IntuyLab)
Project led by: Markus Allmann with Attila Acs, Kyra Bullert, Spela Setzen

1 | Private plot of land in Alto Perú

2 | Community discussion: talking time is the time it takes for a match to burn

3 | Site visit

Alto Perú is an informal settlement on the outskirts of the Chorrillos district in the Peruvian capital Lima. This old part of the city, mainly inhabited by the families of fishermen, has become densified through an extreme influx of families from the hinterland in recent years. Today, the social environment is characterized by a high crime rate, drug dealing, and domestic violence. As in many other urban zones of Lima, an officially registered neighborhood group has been formed to look after the affairs of the settlement. For some years now, a Peruvian-German collective of architects, IntuyLab, based in Lima, and a registered nonprofit organization, Proyecto Alto Perú, have also joined forces to try to improve local conditions, especially for children. In spring 2018, the architects' collective approached the University of Stuttgart with an idea for an international cooperation project in the city. A community center was to be built on the border between historically grown building structures and the informal settlements. This was to offer the neighborhood a venue for meetings and events as well as a safe location for the children of the district to play and learn.

Students of the University of Stuttgart and various Peruvian universities took part in a two-week summer school held by IntuyLab in Lima from late April to early May in 2018. They studied the historical development of Lima, heard talks by local architects and visited existing reference projects. Neighborhood workshops conducted with local partners formed an important part of the summer school. This enabled students to gain an insight into local conditions as well as the needs, difficulties, potentials, and wishes

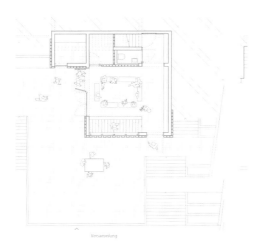

4

Versammlung

5

Bibliothek

of the community living in the urban district. The discussion also served to gather information about spatial requirements. Students took different tours of Alto Perú, intended to give them an opportunity to observe the poor living conditions as well as keep their eyes open for other aspects. How do the people try to improve their way of living, using their own means? What is the local culture and what kinds of building styles are there? How do the people perceive their own lives? To find answers to these questions, the students got in touch with the residents and interviewed them personally. The impressions they gained played an important role in the development of the design.

The spatial program of the building was established in agreement with the neighborhood. It includes a kitchen, a dining room, storage areas, a multipurpose room, a workshop, a library, a child daycare center, and sanitary facilities. During the design process that followed, an intensive exchange took place with the neighborhood on site and with all the cooperation partners, in order to reflect on, discuss, and adapt the design ideas. The final design, which utilizes the distinct topography of the building site across an altitude of about 28 meters, was well approved of in the neighborhood. The planned building is located 10.50 m from the street and embedded in the slope on three levels. By setting the building back from the street, a new, representative public space was created. The first level of the building, flush with the open space in front of it, accommodates a kitchen and dining room with corresponding functional rooms. A workshop, a multipurpose room that can be used for meetings and as a library, and associated side rooms are situated on the second level. The third level of the building contains a child daycare center, including kitchenette and side rooms. The roofs resulting from the stepped design provide additional space for the child daycare center.

Since Peru is subject to earthquakes, the different building parts are separated from each other statically and can move independently in the event of an earthquake. Reinforced concrete is planned for the load-bearing parts, while Peru's traditional building method using loam bricks (adobe) will be implemented otherwise.

Even though the design was well approved by the neighborhood, it could not be implemented so far. The plot is part of a public communal area that the head of the neighborhood group of Alto Perú has declared "untouchable," although he was directly involved in the process since the beginning of the project. The participating institutions had all signed a cooperation agreement. It was eventually revealed that the head of the neighborhood group was pursuing his own interests concerning the plot and thus working against the decisions of the neighborhood. There are speculations regarding what caused this change of mind, but the real reason is not known. Despite extensive preparation and cooperation on site, it has become clear that it is hardly possible for "outsiders" to fully understand the complexity of an informal settlement. The team has therefore learned that social building projects should not be considered as isolated realization projects, but as multilayer processes that can take years until the necessary local structures have been created. In the case of Alto Perú, new channels and strategies are being sought to realize the community center together with the neighborhood after all.

VSB

6

7

fishing harbor

sea wall

- public areas
- sports areas
- occupants of public areas
- trees
- park areas

viewing platform

8

Alto Perú

fish market

private sports club

boat factory

planetarium

4 | Floor plan and usage option as meeting room

5 | Floor plan and usage option as library

6 | Neighborhood in Alto Perú

7 | Sketch for design

8 | Analysis plan of open space in Alto Perú

9 | Analysis plan of usage in Alto Perú

9

- ⁄⁄⁄ historical buildings
- housing
- education
- workshops/small industry
- private sports club
- small businesses
- gastronomy/market
- property
- religious institution
- cultural institution

Alto Perú

Experimental (Re)construction and Northern Cheyenne Resilience

NORTHERN CHEYENNE RESERVATION, MONTANA, USA

CENTER FOR PUBLIC INTEREST DESIGN, PORTLAND STATE UNIVERSITY

Function: Farm building
Size: 200 m²
Building material: Burnt wood

Research phase: 2014–2015
Planning phase: 09.2015–06.2016
Building phase: 07.2016

Students: 30
Further participants on construction site: 24
Lecturers: 3

Client: Sandy and Zane Spang (members of Northern Cheyenne Tribal Council)
Cost: $ 18,000
Financed by: Sandy and Zane Spang (members of Northern Cheyenne Tribal Council)

Project initiated by: Sandy Spang (member of Northern Cheyenne Tribal Council), Sergio Palleroni (Portland State University)
Project led by: Sergio Palleroni (Portland State University), Yuki Takemura (University of Tokyo)

1 | Outside view of new barn with burned forest in background

2 | Front view of new barn

3 | Forest fire behind old barn

Native American reservations are places of great poverty and environmental destruction. Every third inhabitant is presumed to be homeless. Since 1999, Sergio Palleroni, director of the Center for Public Interest Design (CPID), a research institute of Portland State University in Oregon, has started various initiatives in Native American reservations, including two projects that resulted from a larger research project.

The first of these is a straw bale house program. Straw is a local, quickly renewable raw material that can also be used as a building material. Students had already constructed single-story houses in reservations in Montana and South Dakota under the supervision of Palleroni back in 1998. Accompanied by phases of intensive research on the safety and durability of straw constructions, further projects were conducted in the Northern Cheyenne Reservation, such as a two-story house, a child daycare facility, and a training center at Chief Dull Knife College. In the course of this, it proved to be ideal for 15 to 20 students to be on location for one week before construction of a straw bale house. This allows them to get to know the potential users and their needs and gain a better understanding of the context. In the next step, students develop building designs in cooperation with the clients. Student activities during the following semester include execution planning work, efforts to gain the support of the community and safeguard financing, as well as ordering materials.

The bales of straw are structural components of the houses. Wood is only used for the foundation and roof construction. The walls consist entirely of bales of straw, which also carry the roof load. An

EMERGENCY OPERATION

How emergency response system worked in ash creek fire

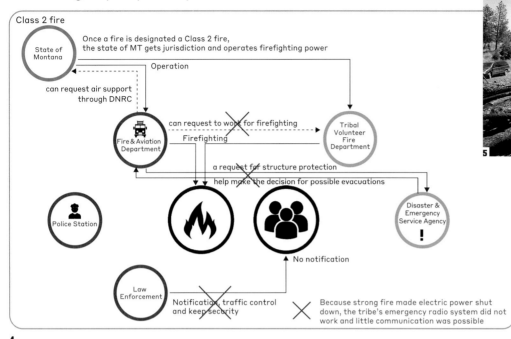
5

Class 2 fire

State of Montana

Once a fire is designated a Class 2 fire, the state of MT gets jurisdiction and operates firefighting power

Operation

can request air support through DNRC

Fire & Aviation Department

can request to work for firefighting

Firefighting

Tribal Volunteer Fire Department

a request for structure protection

help make the decision for possible evacuations

Police Station

Disaster & Emergency Service Agency
!

No notification

Law Enforcement

Notification, traffic control and keep security

Because strong fire made electric power shut down, the tribe's emergency radio system did not work and little communication was possible

4

outer layer of breathable plastering prevents moisture from entering the walls of the house from the kitchen or bathroom, for example, which would facilitate biological decomposition of the straw bales. The pressed bales contain little oxygen, making the houses extensively fire-resistant – an important factor in an area frequently affected by forest fires. Part of the program is that the students teach the building method to the people living in the reservation, so as to both alleviate the acute shortage of housing and create jobs at the same time. The building method's minimal need for professional craftsmen is a major advantage.

The second important measure followed in 2012, the year in which catastrophic forest fires ravaged the tribal lands of the Northern Cheyenne. Following decades of drought, almost 40% of the reservation was in flames within hours. Many tribe members lost all they had. The tribe approached the CPID with a request to work out an action plan designed to better prepare the Cheyenne for the impacts of climate change.

The CPID started with research on improved land management methods and how this would affect the community and its administration. A series of site surveys, interviews, and discussions were carried out by the students to identify weaknesses as well as determine solutions and financing opportunities. Research showed that stable communication methods were lacking: cooperation between the tribal leaders and the Bureau of Native American Affairs was strained and regulations in the event of a catastrophe

did not exist. Available emergency accommodation were not adequate. Most importantly, it was necessary to create a housing construction program in order to improve the already precarious living conditions of tribe members, which had been aggravated by the fires. An analysis of what had or hadn't proven to be effective in the case of a catastrophe was turned into a resilience plan, which not only contained a guideline for mastering future crises, but also suggestions for a sustainable development of the reservation.

The CPID conducted a series of different projects, including one on building with wood from fire-damaged trees. PhD students of the CPID and other faculties first built a lumber mill in the reservation to process fire-damaged wood. In dialogue with the tribe members, the CPID students then proceeded to design a building to be constructed with this wood. This was to serve as a prototype for reconstruction of the destroyed farm buildings. The building work was carried out together with the members of the tribe, who can now use their newly acquired skills to rebuild other structures lost by the fires.

VSB

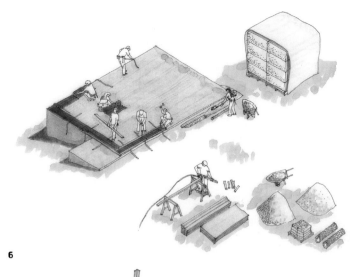

6

12

13

7

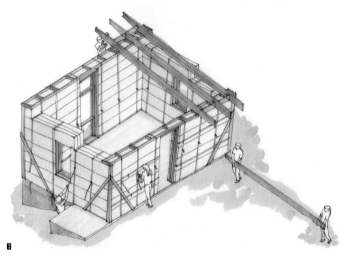

8

9

11

10

4 | Analysis of consequences of power failure

5 | Removal of the fire damaged logs for processing into construction timber

6–10 | Sketches relating to building process of straw bale house

11 | Interior of straw bale house

12 + 13 | Building process of straw bale house

Quiané DesignBuild Studio

SANTA CATARINA QUIANÉ, OAXACA, MEXICO

MUNICH UNIVERSITY OF APPLIED SCIENCES

Function: Center for Culture and Ecology
Size: 200 m² (building), 200 m² (exterior area)
Building material: Reinforced concrete (base), timber (roof structure), loam (infill), polyethylene (roof panels)

Research phase: 10.2018–11.2018
Design phase: 09.04.2019–24.01.2018
Building phase: 09.04.2019–10.03.2018

Students: 21 students of Munich University of Applied Sciences (MUAS), 3 students of Universidad La Salle, Oaxaca
Further participants on construction site: 3–12
Lecturers: 5

Client: Municipality of Santa Catarina Quiané
Cost: EUR 25,000 (building material), EUR 6,000 (tools)
Financed by: miscellaneous

Project initiated by: Ursula Hartig (MUAS) in cooperation with CAMPO A.C.
Project led by: Ursula Hartig with Lorena Burbano, Sebastián Oviedo, Ferdinand Loserth, Jörg Jungwirth (MUAS)

1 | Folding doors leading
to hall

2 | Critical consider-
ation of design with
students

3 | Dinner on the
building site

The Center for Culture and Ecology is a project in the small municipality of Santa Catarina Quiané, located approximately 485 km southeast of Mexico City. The town is part of the Federal State of Oaxaca, which is one of the poorest regions of Mexico and faces problems such as unemployment, rural depopulation, loss of cultural identity, lacking perspectives for young people, as well as earthquakes. In addition, there is a conflict with the capital city of the federal state, which is buying more and more property in the municipality in order to build housing for government employees. This process poses a threat to the cultural heritage of the rural population.

Although the municipality has a well-organized civil society and a lively culture, it has no premises for their activities. The idea to build a Center for Culture and Ecology in the municipality was the result of an initiative by Ursula Hartig, Professor of Planning and Building in a Global Context at the Munich University of Applied Sciences, in cooperation with the municipality and the Mexican non-government organization CAMPO.

The partners developed a spatial concept together. Diverse usage requirements demanded features such as several halls, toilets and showers, workshops, a sewage treatment plant, cisterns, a meeting area, and a municipal kitchen. The students developed the design and execution planning of the center during the winter semester of 2018/2019. Since it was not possible to realize everything in one go, implementation in several building phases was opted for. One of the halls and the sanitary building with a small sewage treatment plant were built within the first

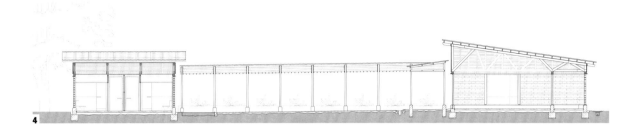

of the five weeks allocated for building work. The load-bearing structure of the walls is made up of a grid of timber posts, anchored in a concrete base and infilled with locally produced loam bricks. Recycled Tetra Paks were used to make panels for covering the roof. The connection of the two buildings creates a covered gallery, offering protection from sun and rain. A garden with local succulents is located towards the eastern end of the grounds.

The collaboration between the university of applied sciences, the town community, and CAMPO called for special communication methods. The NGO's directors discussed on site with members of the municipality what they thought the future center should be like, and moderated between them and the students by means of video conferences. CAMPO provided the municipality with plans during the course of the design process and made sure that the students received feedback. Communication was based on photographs, videos, pictograms, as well as drawings and models made by the students. A phase plan was finally developed by all the parties involved. Besides the building plan, this also included points such as the students' accommodations and catering and the extent of financial resources and contributions in kind to be raised.

A completely different form of communication was practiced among the students. First of all, a basis for communication between architecture and civil engineering students had to be established. They were familiarized with the technical principles regarding the use of loam and timber as well as earthquake-proof building in jointly attended workshops at the University of Applied Sciences. Experiences of students who

had learned a trade before their academic studies were also made use of. Building processes of individual trades, such as foundation, masonry, or timber structure, were studied in specific groups. This division of labor proved to be successful on site, since responsibility was distributed to the entire group in this way. The skills of four qualified carpenters and joiners also turned out to be very useful for the timber construction components of the project.

Local laborers additionally helped with the building work. An exchange, for example, took place with a loam builder who showed the students the local adobe building method. Piping was laid and toilets and showers were installed in the sanitary building in close collaboration with local craftsmen.

Another decisive factor for the realization of the project was the great commitment of the students in Munich, who helped to raise the necessary funds. They managed to secure over half of the total budget from companies, institutions, and private persons by means of solicitation letters, donation flyers, newspaper articles, and a charity concert. The students finally published a book and presented the outcome to other students and the general public in an exhibition at the University of Applied Sciences.

SBA

4 | Section of sanitary block and hall

5 | Roofing between hall and sanitary block

6 | Windows of hall and projecting roof

7

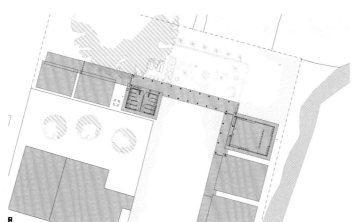

8

9

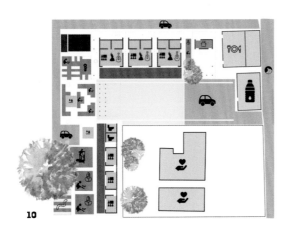

10

7 | Site plan

8 | Floor plan of first
building phase

9 | Masonry workshop
at Munich University of
Applied Sciences

10 | Simplified graphic
explaining usage of the
building to the com-
munity

Community Center Spinelli

TECHNICAL UNIVERSTIY OF KAISERSLAUTERN

Function: Community center and retreat
Size: 550 m²
Building material: Wood (spruce and Douglas fir)

Research phase: 11.2015–03.2016
Planning phase: 04.2016–07.2016
Building phase: 08.2016–11.2016

Students: 18
Further participants on construction site: approx. 25
Lecturers: 5

Client: State of Baden-Württemberg; City of Mannheim
Cost: approx. EUR 210,000 (monetary and non-monetary resources)
Financed by: State of Baden-Württemberg, City of Mannheim, financial donations, and in-kind contributions from: Spax, Festool, Daimler, Fama, Ruben, Hornbach, Bauen für Orange Farm, and various private donors

Project initiated by: Tatjana Dürr, Stefan Krötsch (TU Kaiserslautern)
Project led by: Stefan Krötsch, Andreas Kretzer, Jürgen Graf (TU Kaiserslautern)

1 | Group effort for roof girder

2 | Inner courtyard with seating

3 | Prefabrication of wall elements

The number of refugees seeking shelter in Germany rose dramatically in the late summer of 2015. In order to accommodate as many people as possible, an initial reception center (Landeserstaufnahme-einrichtung – LEA) was created in the Spinelli Barracks on the former military grounds located in the north-east of Mannheim. It soon became clear that the existing storage buildings would have to serve as provisional housing for a longer period of time. Facilities such as communal areas and places for retreat, which were urgently needed in this critical situation, were not available. The fact that the accommodation were located far away from the city on socially disconnected and dismal barracks grounds made it all the more important to provide a place for people to meet.

This led to the idea of creating an inviting community center for the refugees. A great variety of actors were involved in the realization of the project: the state government that largely financed the project, the Building Competence Center of the City of Mannheim, students and lecturers at TU Kaiserslautern, residents of the initial reception center and local craftsmen and suppliers.

The refugees' participation in the planning and building process was intended from the start. Their involvement in the project gave them an opportunity to actively influence the surroundings of the accommodations, even though they themselves would presumably not get to experience the built result anymore. All the participants were of course aware of the fact that the time spent in such an

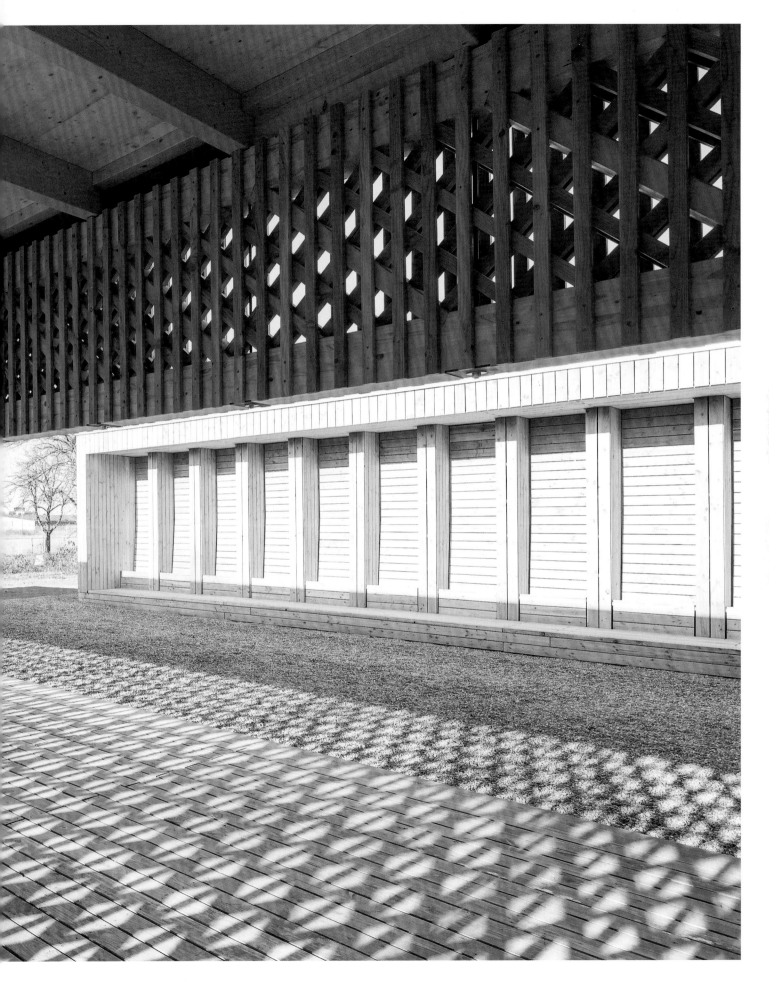

initial reception center is limited. Working with the students and craftsmen, however, allowed them to improve their German, learn new building-related skills, familiarize themselves with typical German workflows, and make friends. The 18 students from TU Kaiserslautern who planned the community center over a period of four months and built it together with the refugees in another four months were naturally also able to gain positive experiences.

Together with Tatjana Dürr, Officer for Building Culture of the City of Mannheim, three students of the Department of Architecture at TU Kaiserslautern, Stefan Krötsch, Jürgen Graf, and Andreas Kretzer, developed a concept for the student building project. In a joint workshop, a spatial program was developed, which the students then transformed into an architectural design. The special feature of the design is the way in which the interior and exterior spaces merge with each other. The walls of the main building continue into the exterior space towards the north, creating two inner courtyards intended to serve different requirements: an enclosed yard with covered seating niches towards the east and south provides a place for private retreat and reading. Seating areas oriented to the south and west surround a large yard for events, suitable for communal activities such as sports, meals, and diverse events. The communal room faces this yard, allowing it to be used as a stage for events. The design vocabulary used for the community center is reminiscent of North African ornamentation, with transparent, lattice-like wooden walls forming an attractive pattern familiar from the architecture in the refugees' home countries. The construction is designed to allow it to be built by hand, without the need for major equipment. The dialogue between students and refugees commenced in the design phase and was a conceptual prerequisite. They also lived in the same premises during the construction period and received the same food and drink. Correspondingly close group dynamics developed between the participants. It was ultimately a communal building process, which, after completion the refugees described as having been essential. Their labour was for others, but the time spent taking part in the project was more important than the result.

SBA

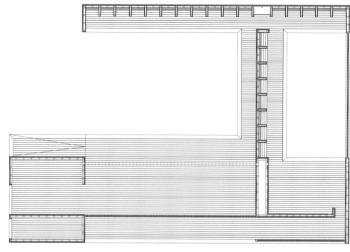

5

6

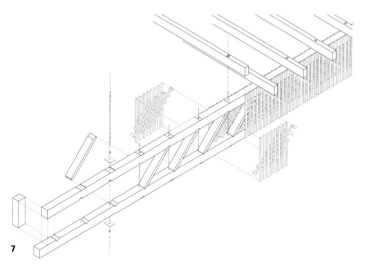

7

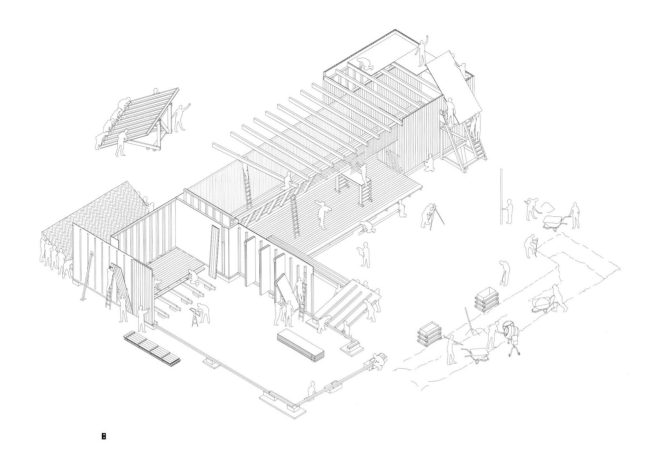

8

9

4 | Larger inner
courtyard

5 | Floor plan

6 | Many hands instead
of large machines

7 | Exploded axono-
metric view of roof
girder

8 | Axonometric
representation of
building process

9 | Large inner
courtyard with seating

Maison pour tous (House for All)

FOUR, FRANCE

Function: Community center
Size: 150 m²
Building material: Zinc, reinforced concrete, rammed earth, wood fiber, charred wood, spruce and larch wood

Research phase: 09.2017
Planning phase: 10.2017
Building phase: 03.2018–09.2018

Students: 22
Further participants on construction site: approx. 24
Lecturers: 2

Client: Municipality of Four
Cost: EUR 575,000
Financed by: Municipality of Four and sponsors

Project initiated by: Municipality of Four, Grenoble School of Architecture (ENSAG)
Project led by: Marie and Keith Zawistowski (design/buildLAB)

1 | Rammed earth children's workshop

2 | Image of interior of multifunctional room

3 | Residents discuss student designs

Maison pour tous (House for All) is a project by the municipality of Four, situated southeast of Lyon in the Auvergne-Rhône-Alpes region. The population of Four has increased significantly due to the influx of people from surrounding areas in recent years. The construction of a "house for all" expresses the municipality's endeavor to be actively involved in future development. The aim was to create a meeting place for people of different origins that could also be used by 20 sports clubs and even by residents of the surrounding towns and villages.

The municipality asked the design/buildLAB of the École nationale supérieure d'architecture de Grenoble (ENSAG – Grenoble School of Architecture) for support in realization of the project. Research for the project started in early September 2017. The students traveled to Four in order to find out about the requirements and conditions on location. The scope of the project and expectations of local stakeholders were discussed in a first meeting with selected officials and representatives of local organizations. The students then produced 11 sketches and invited the residents of Four to inspect them at the end of September 2017. Suggestions and criticisms were incorporated in six new sketches by the students, which were again shown to the municipality and local interest groups. In a third meeting, the result of the consultation process was presented in the form of a final sketch.

The next stage involved overcoming the obstacles of the building permit process, which is prescribed by French building legislation for design projects by students. To this end, the administration of the region

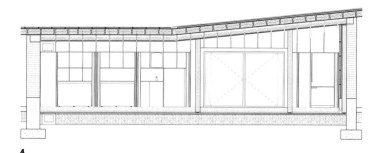

4

5

Auvergne-Rhône-Alpes provided legal expertise for the students and the municipality.

Another challenge for the students was to develop an ecologically responsible, sustainable building using local, natural materials. Apart from the easily recyclable zinc for the roof and the concrete using local aggregate for the foundation and supporting structures of the building as well as for the terrace construction, loam and wood were predominantly used. The municipality of Four is situated in the department de l'Isère. The people of this region have known about the suitability of their soil for rammed earth constructions for centuries. Its use and integration in the realization of the project not only aims to enhance sustainability but also showcase a modern and innovative application. Locally sourced wood was used for the roof construction as well as for cladding the facades of the two adjoining buildings. The technique of controlled burning of the outer layers of wood was implemented to make the wood of the facades more durable. Charring creates a natural protective layer preventing damage of the material through pests, climate, and humidity.

The House for All is divided into three architectural units, which blend into the environment harmoniously: a multifunctional space built using loam with large, folding doors, a wooden, flexibly divisible storage room, and a sanitary block, also made of wood. The buildings frame a courtyard oriented to the west, with a bench and a deciduous tree forming an oasis of peace. An extensive space to the north can be used for major outdoor events. Games on the adjacent football pitch can be watched from an elevated platform to the east. A hill in the south offers space for children to play. Large roof overhangs, designed in line with the course of the sun, passively warm up or shade the main hall and create a link to the adjoining buildings.

While the students exchanged ideas with the lecturing architects for the design, they were split up and assigned to different trades on the construction site, with the firms incorporating them in their construction teams as apprentices, as it were. The building was therefore constructed by the students together with professional craftsmen and assisting community members. This ensured static and structural safety of the building as well as facilitating an exchange of knowledge and experience between the future architects, the client, the craftsmen, and members of the community.

VSB

4 | Section of
multifunctional room

5 | View of the building

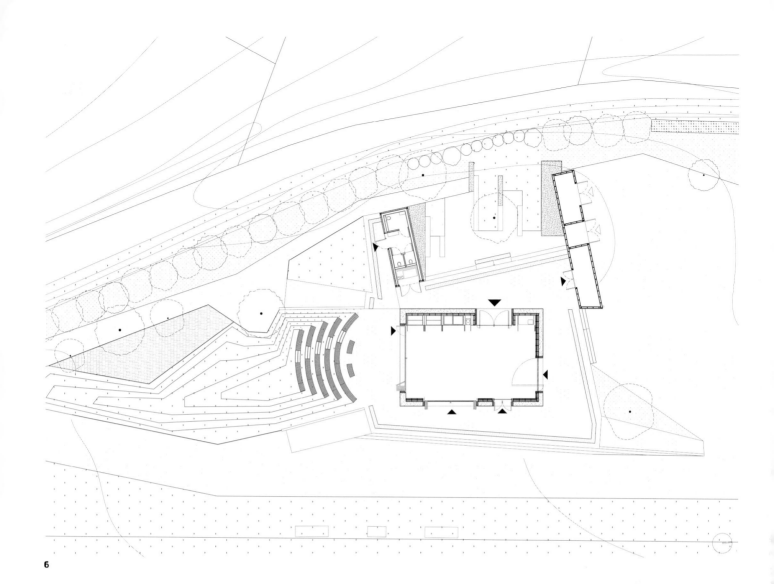

6

7

8

6 | Floor plan of complex

7 | Creation of rammed
earth wall

8 | View of complex

Student Housing

SAN MIGUEL DE LOS COLORADOS, JUJUY, ARGENTINA

3

Function: Student housing
Size: 52 m²
Building material: Adobe loam bricks, stone foundation

Research phase: Beginning of 2016
Planning phase: 10.2016
Building phase: 12.2016–06.2017

Students: 8
Lecturers: 12

Client: Escuela secundaria N° 51, San Miguel de los Colorados
Cost: not specified
Financed by: Private companies and community

Project initiated by: Amiguito del Norte and UM FADAU
Project led by: Alejandro Borrachia

1 | Completed student dormitory

2 | The domes are plastered

3 | View of school complex with student housing in the background

FACULTY OF ARCHITECTURE, DESIGN, ART AND URBANISM (FADAU), UNIVERSITY OF MORÓN

Like many schools of architecture in South America, the Faculty of Architecture, Design, Art and Urbanism (FADAU) of the University of Morón (UM), Buenos Aires, has required students to participate in a Design-Build project in order to obtain their graduate degree since 2016. This gives students an opportunity to develop a social project in their country in collaboration with various players and institutions. It also familiarizes them with the parallel world shaped by extreme poverty prevailing in their country. The focus is particularly on people living in the countryside rather than on those in big cities.

This also applied to a project initiated by students of the FADAU in San Miguel de los Colorados, a place in the province of Jujuy in the far northwest of Argentina, at an altitude of around 3,800 m. The province has major social, economic, ecological, as well as urban-planning problems, which led the FADAU students to work out a model for sustainable urban and architectural development. They realized one of the modules that had been requested by the Amiguito del Norte Foundation and the community of San Miguel de los Colorados: accommodations with sanitary facilities and a kitchen for the students of the local secondary school (Escuela secundaria N° 51). The architecture students visited the community and obtained information about its requirements and the local situation. They found out that some pupils had to walk on mountain paths for about four hours to get to school, which is impossible on bad-weather days. Many pupils had dropped out of school due to the knowledge

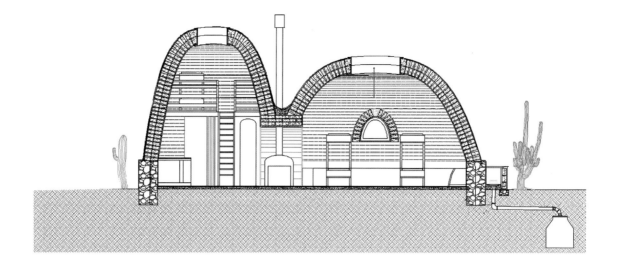

4

gaps resulting from this. Therefore, the plan was to design a structure offering pupils the possibility to stay at school in the future. This was to make sure that they could attend class every day.

Eight students from the FADAU subsequently designed two interconnected domes, which reflect the morphology of the surrounding mountains. One of them, with a floor space of 42 m², was intended for the pupils to sleep in, while the other one was reserved for the kitchen and sanitary facilities. The students presented their concept to the community and incorporated their modification requests. Further discussions were held to clarify questions concerning the plot of land, supply of local materials, participation of community members, material transport logistics, and accommodation of the FADAU students on site. The buildings were constructed from self-made loam bricks. These help with energy efficiency by preventing the development

of extreme temperatures in the rooms both in summer and winter. The domes are rounded off with an opening, allowing daylight to enter the rooms and thereby making further lighting unnecessary. A purpose-built, radially rotatable structure was set up on the inside of the stone domes to arrange the stones so as to achieve the desired shape. This tool can also be used by the community members for other buildings. Furthermore, the design was kept deliberately simple and hence easily reproducible. This fulfilled one of the goals that the students had set for themselves: to train the actively participating community members in the new building method and enable them to construct more buildings with this technique, so that they could complete the master plan independently.

VSB

4 | Section of student dormitory

5 | Floor plan of dormitory

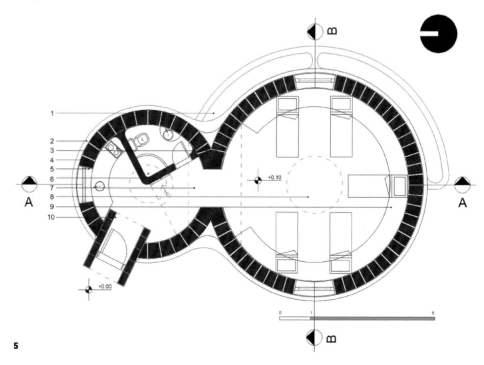

5

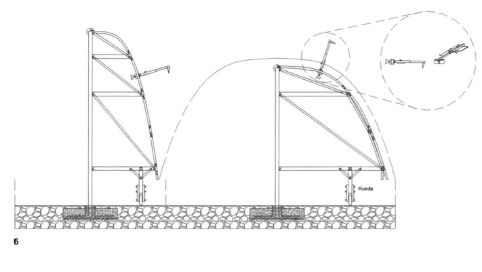

6

7

8

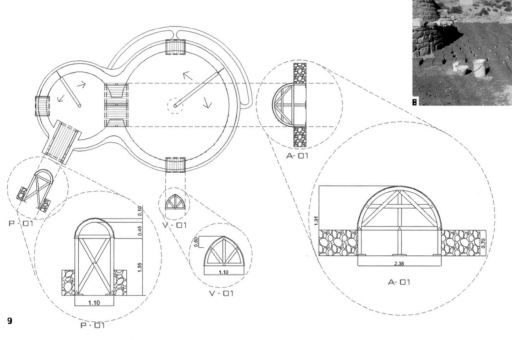

A-01

P-01

V-01

V-01

A-01

9

10

6 | Device designed
by the students for the
construction of the domes

7 | Interior view of the
completed dormitory

8 | Clay stones laid out
to dry on the construction
site

9 | Functional mechanism
of the self-made device
for the construction of
the domes

10 | Completed student
dormitory

Guga S'Thebe Theater

CAPE TOWN, SOUTH AFRICA

PBSA DÜSSELDORF HSD
RWTH AACHEN;
GEORGIA TECH, ATLANTA;
CS STUDIO ARCHITECTS CAPE TOWN;
IMAGINE STRUCTURE,
FRANKFURT A.M./COLOGNE

Function: Theater, cultural center
Size: 560 m²
Building material: Steel, timber, lightweight loam, bricks

Research phase: 2012–2013
Planning phase: 2013–2015
Building phase: 2013–2015

Students: approx. 300
Further participants on construction site: approx. 40
Lecturers: 18
Cooperations: Transsolar, Stuttgart;
University of Cape Town (UCT); Detmold School of Architecture and Interior Architecture

Client: City of Cape Town
Cost: EUR 130,000
Financed by: Bischöflicher Hilfsfonds Eine Welt (charity organization), Ein Herz für Kinder – Bild hilft e.V.; Interstuhl Büromöbel; Karl Bröcker Foundation; Rotary Clubs Berlin-Gedächtniskirche and Munich; Rudolf-August Oetker Foundation; Steven A. Denning Award, Sto Foundation, and numerous sponsors from the building industry and architecture

Project initiated by: AIT ArchitekturSalon
Project led by: Daniel Baerlecken (Georgia Institute of Technology), Bernadette Heiermann, Nora Müller (RWTH Aachen), Judith Reitz (Peter Behrens School of Arts)

1 | Fitting the facade

2 | Finished theater building

3 | Theater performance on the building site

A lot may have changed in one of South Africa's largest cities, Cape Town, since the end of apartheid, yet millions of people are still living in very basic township settlements. The Guga S'Thebe Arts and Cultural Center in Langa, the oldest township of the city, was built back in 1999. It attracts locals, children, young people, and artists from the surrounding areas as well as tourists from all over the world. The center lacked a building offering space for art, concerts, theater, and dance performances, especially for children and young people. This is how the idea came about to build a theater within the scope of a DesignBuild project, as a new component of the cultural center. Students at five universities of applied sciences designed, planned, and built a modular multifunctional space over a period of three years and five building phases. Apart from members of the universities of applied sciences and relevant experts, the process involved neighbors, users, representatives of culture and politics, and the local heritage foundation.

Planning and realization focused on the use of local, traditional, and recycled materials, in combination with innovative low-tech building methods. At the end of the first planning phase, the students decided to make use of 11 overseas containers that could be acquired at a good price by auction in the port of Cape Town. During the first building phases, a space accommodating an audience of approximately 200 people was created in spring 2013 by staggered stacking of the containers. The partially cut-open containers provided space for a backstage area, central control room, sound studio, kitchen, and offices. A shed roof made of wood is supported by an independent steel structure. Nail plate trusses, commonly used in South African industrial building, are joined to form an open web-like V-structure. This signature feature of the exterior is also visible from the inside.

As soon as the interior space was covered by a roof, it was used as a place for rehearsals, performances, and exhibitions. This made it possible to leave the further course of the design development open for the next two years. During four further building phases, most of the decisions regarding finishing and the facade were made on site, material was looked for in local scrapyards, and 1:1 components were tested on the building. The individual universities of applied sciences were on site successively for periods between eight and twelve weeks. Each group reacted to the specifications of the preceding group and continued to develop the building tasks in close agreement with everyone involved.

High-quality external cladding of the container architecture was planned right from the start. This was to express the great appreciation for the cultural events taking place inside as well as for the informal settlement located behind the theater – a garment entirely in line with Semper's theory of dressing. The ultimately realized facade fulfills the requirement of providing insulating weather protection by means of modules consisting of used transport pallets and a mixture of compacted straw and loam made on site, while at the same time making use of various traditional ornaments. The outer facade level that determines the overall appearance of the building is a textural adaptation of shoowa cloth, which originates from Congo but is also found in the Cape region. The

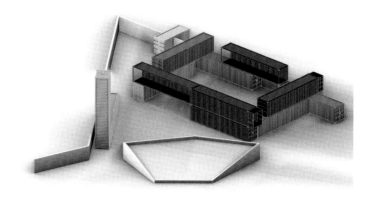

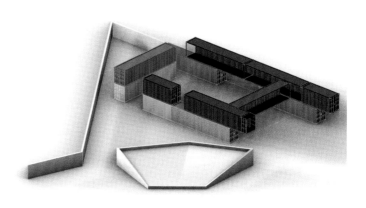

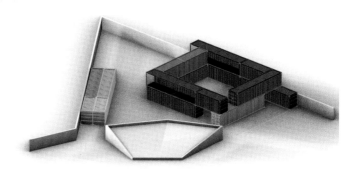

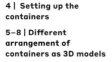

4 | Setting up the containers

5–8 | Different arrangement of containers as 3D models

5–8

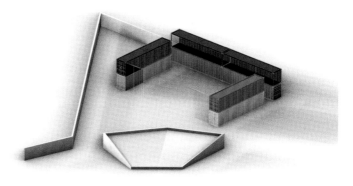

irregular zigzag pattern typical of these textiles is reflected by the arrangement of partly colored, vertical wooden panels taken from recycled fruit crates. The side of the theater facing the informal settlement was clad with a brick wall, the relief-like structure of which also calls to mind woven textiles.

The interior space is decorated with hexagonal floor tiles, partly fitted with mosaics, which were cast by the students, together with artists and young people from Langa, using self-made frames. The window bars made of used steel parts are a graphic reflection of the shoowa pattern. Textiles and acoustic elements on the walls were created in a workshop with local and international artists. The changing works of art result from the impression that the design of the theater is subject to constant alteration.

SBA

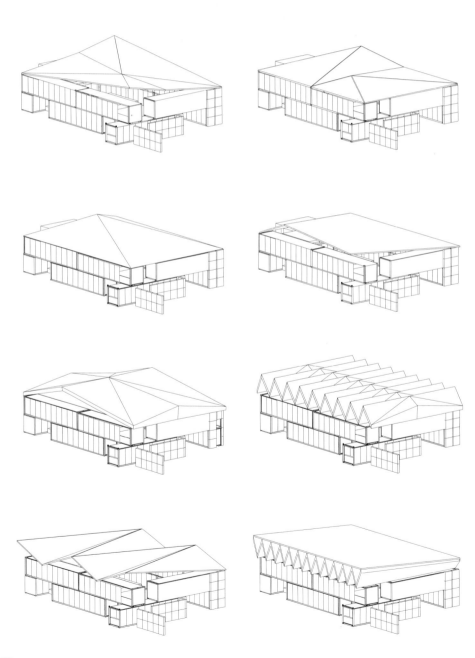

9 | Installing roof supporting structure on container

10 | Different roof varieties as 3D models

10

11

12

13

14

15

11 | Facade design

12 | Preparation of
recycled wooden facade
elements

13 | Insulating elements
made of straw-loam
mixture and wooden
facade elements

14 | Finished facade

15 | Insulating elements
and brick wall

16 | Image of interior of theater hall interior

17 | Kitchen with counter adjoining theater hall

18 | Gallery on first floor

19 | Floor plan with floor mosaic

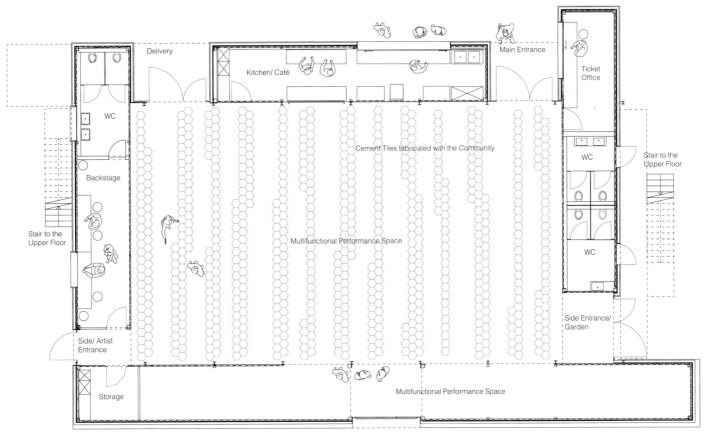

Delivery

Kitchen/ Café

Main Entrance

Ticket Office

WC

Cement Tiles fabricated with the Community

Stair to the Upper Floor

Backstage

WC

Stair to the Upper Floor

WC

Multifunctional Performance Space

Side/ Artist Entrance

Side Entrance/ Garden

Storage

Multifunctional Performance Space

19

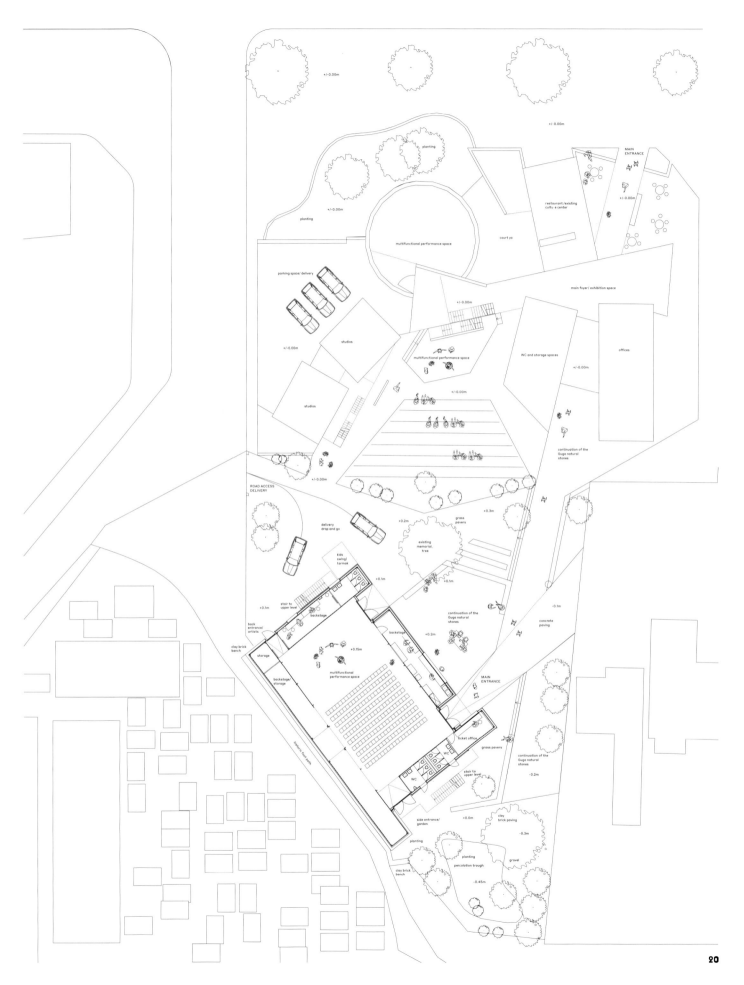

MAIN
ENTRANCE

+/-0.00m

planting

+/-0.00m

planting

restaurant /existing
cultu e center

court ya

multifunctional performance space

main foyer/ exhibition space

parking space/ delivery

+/-0.00m

multifunctional performance space

WC and storage spaces

offices

studios

+/-0.00m

+/-0.00m

studios

continuation of the
Guga natural
stones

ROAD ACCESS
DELIVERY

+/-0.00m

+0.2m

grass
pavers

+0.3m

delivery
drop and go

existing
memorial
tree

kids
swing/
tarmak

+0.1m

+0.1m

-0.1m

+0.1m

stair to
upper level

backstage

continuation of the
Guga natural
stones

concrete
paving

back
entrance/
artists

backstage

+0.2m

clay brick
bench

+0.15m

storage

MAIN
ENTRANCE

backstage/
storage

multifunctional
performance space

ticket office

WC

grass pavers

continuation of the
Guga natural
stones

WC

-0.2m

stair to
upper level

side entrance/
garden

+0.0m

clay
brick paving

planting

-0.3m

clay brick
bench

planting

gravel

percolation trough

-0.45m

20

20 | Landscape archi-
tecture plan of exterior

21 | Residents wash in
front of the building

22 | Aerial photograph
of complex)

2019 Jim Vlock Building Project

NEW HAVEN, CONNECTICUT, USA

YALE SCHOOL OF ARCHITECTURE, YALE UNIVERSITY

Function: House with three units
Size: 150 m²
Building material: Concrete (foundations), wood

Research phase: 6 weeks
Design phase: 8 weeks
Building phase: 15 weeks

Students: 57
Further participants on construction site: 2 faculty members, 1 associate professor
Subcontractors: excavation, electrotechnology, plumbing, heating, drywalling
Lecturers: 5

Client: Columbus House, New Haven

Cost: EUR 200,000
Financed by: Columbus House, New Haven; Yale School of Architecture; contributions from various building trades

Project initiated by: Columbus House
Project led by: Adam Hopfner (Yale School of Architecture)

1 | Model of a design

2 | Loggia of finished building

3 | Exterior view of finished residential building

DesignBuild has been a component of architectural education at the Yale School of Architecture since 1967. Charles W. Moore, director of the School of Architecture from 1965 to 1971, and Kent Bloomer introduced these First-year Building Projects for Master's students. Students take part in a Design-Build project within the first of three academic years – which is in fact compulsory. It can be considered as a reaction by Moore to student protests and increasing politicization on campus at the end of the 1970s. He took the students' discontent as an opportunity to get socially involved, together with the students, and to build for people living in poverty. Projects were realized throughout the USA during the first ten years. Since the 1970s, the Building Project has been focusing on residential buildings in neglected urban districts of New Haven. Around a quarter of the population lives below the poverty line there. Various cooperations with organizations promoting social building and neighborhood help have made it possible to create affordable living space for around 50 families.

2019 marked the third collaboration of the Yale School with Columbus House, an organization supporting families affected by homelessness. The task of the first-year Master's students was to design a residential building with three units in the southern urban district The Hill. At the beginning of the semester, the whole year was divided into teams that developed initial designs, supervised by five lecturers. First, the students examined the dimensional limits of dwelling space to determine the essential

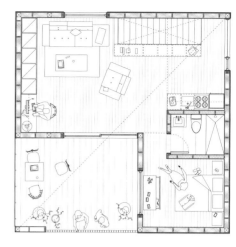

4–6

spatial, ergonomic, functional, and emotional mea-sures of human habitation. Second, the students focused on the material enclosure assembly that would encompass the interior domestic space. Third, the students developed a system by which an individ-ual dwelling unit was equipped to accommodate three parties within a single building envelope. And fourth, the students had to reconcile the building with a particular urban infill site, and to accommodate the environmental and built context.

The prevailing proposal was based on the architec-ture of the "triple decker," characteristic of New Haven: three stacked floors, each with a separate entrance and veranda, yet externally forming a unit as a house. Taking up this typology, the students designed an L-shaped layout on a square area of 72.5 m², which is reproduced on each floor, but with a 90-degree rotation. The two required staircases are situated on the inside along the southern and east-ern edge of the apartments, different from the typ-ical triple-decker housing, with exterior stairs and verandas.

The layout includes an open kitchen and living room, a bedroom, a storeroom, and a small sanitary block located at the rear of the kitchen cabinets, thereby separating the living from the sleeping area. A large glass sliding door opens the living rooms to the square terraces. Residents can also make a little garden out of these 14 m² outside areas. At the same time, the opening to the living room as well as to the bedroom provides generous illumination, so that the apartment only required three additional windows.

The organization of the kitchen and sanitary block as a standardized unit, named "power cell" by the students, is an essential characteristic of the inte-rior layout. This also features wall closets designed by the students, extending from the kitchen cabinets around the corner to the bathroom door. The wooden closets provide important storage space, making it unnecessary to buy furniture for storage privately. Additionally, each apartment has an individual store-room situated under the stairs on the two lower floors. The design makes use of compact organized areas to facilitate – comparatively – generous living spaces and outside areas.

The building phase started in June 2019 and was scheduled for four months. Designed as a timber con-struction, the students had no difficulties in erecting the building without major equipment. The construc-tion is stabilized by isolated steel girders. The facade was clad with black pickled wooden strips on all sides. A strict horizontality is counteracted by differently sized windows and terraces, on whose sides the facade opens up in the form of slats, allowing light to pass through and screening from view. This integrates the house in the visual appearance of the neighbor-hood facades, while also distancing itself through its coloring and construction details.

SBA

7

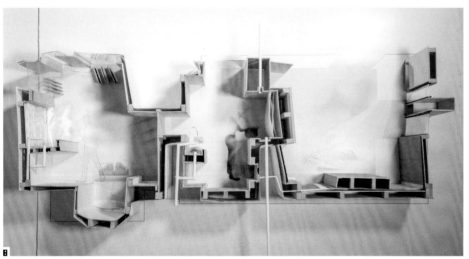

8

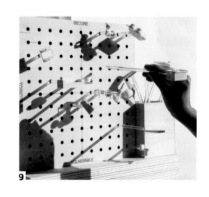

9

10

11

4–6 | Left: Floor plan of ground floor
Center: Floor plan of 1st floor
Right: Floor plan of 2nd floor

7–10 | Conceptual design models and spatial analyses

11 | Interior view of completed building

Kitchen on the Run

MOBILE PAVILION

Function: Pavilion for communal cooking and eating – integration incubator
Size: L 6.04 m, W 2.38 m, H 2.97 m
Building material: Wood, steel, plastic

Planning phase: 10.2015–01.2016
Building phase: 01.2016–02.2016

Students: 19
Further participants on construction site: 5
Lecturers: 4

Client: Kitchen on the Run/Über den Tellerrand e.V.
Cost: EUR 17,500 (building costs), EUR 7,000 (donations for equipment)
Financed by: Mercator Foundation, Sto Foundation, Hans Sauer Foundation, and other donors

Project initiated by: Rabea Haß, Jule Schröder, Andreas Reinhard
Project led by: Donatella Fioretti, Marc Benjamin Drewes, Simon Mahringer, Christoph Rokitta (TU Berlin); Über den Tellerrand e.V. (client)

1 | Furnished, completed kitchen

2 | Model of container with terrace and furniture

3, 4 | Side view with attached terrace and open container door

As ever more refugees came to Europe in the spring of 2015, Rabea Haß and Jule Schröder asked themselves how locals and refugees could meet and get to know each other, in an effort to reduce the preconceptions that existed on both sides. After coming up with the idea of a mobile kitchen, they joined Über den Tellerrand, a Berlin-based association that combines culinary, creative, and sports events through a friendly network of people with and without a refugee background. The intention was to allow refugees and local people to get to know each other a little more while cooking and eating together. Their idea won one of ten prizes in the Advocate Europe competition, which provided them with initial funding. When they contacted Donatella Fioretti's Chair of Architectural Design and Construction at TU Berlin to ask about the possibility of realizing the idea within the context of a DesignBuild project, they received a positive reply.

The students were given the task of transforming a freight container into a space for communal cooking, offering a generously sized work area, storage, and space for up to 25 persons, while at the same time creating a homely, cosy atmosphere. An additional requirement was that the structure could be built by hand by only a few persons within one day and that it would function reliably on the move. During the first phase of a three-week competition, students paired up to work out proposals for the conversion of the container. The jury of the competition, made up of

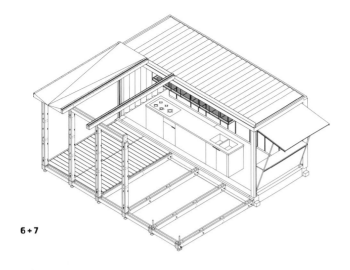
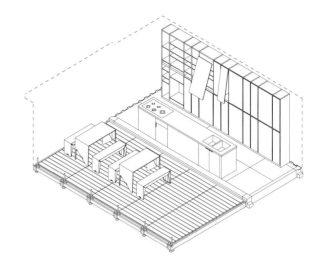

6 + 7

lecturers and the initiators, selected the best ideas from the various contributions and asked the students to combine these in a complete design.

The second phase was dedicated to collectively developing the design of the final project. The students were also required to contact various material manufacturers and try to win these as sponsors.

The kitchen units form the heart of the project's final plan. The container opens up on two sides from this central point. In order to enlarge the usable floor space, a terrace made up of supports and girders can be attached to the long, openable sides of the container. Flooring elements can be hooked into this wooden skeleton construction and a roof skin made of segmented lorry tarpaulin. The segments are folded and form an inclined, almost sculptural roof structure. The opened container doors serve as side walls. A small bar counter that functions as a kiosk can be folded out on the narrow side to the right. Folding it out fully creates another access to the kitchen.

Multifunctionality is the criterion that also determines the other elements of the interior. This applies in particular to the furniture designed by the students. The simple origami-like tables and benches made of lightweight particleboard can be folded and serve as the front of a ceiling-high wooden shelf when folded up. The shelf extends across the entire rear wall of the container. All eating, cooking, and work utensils can be stored there. A structure made of round steel bars can be suspended above the entire length of the cooking area, which includes a gas stove, an oven, and two sinks. As in classical restaurant kitchens, this provides plenty of storage space and places for conveniently hanging up cooking utensils. A hose with a sprayer attachment runs across the ceiling of the container and can be attached to a water tap wherever required in the mobile kitchen.

The third phase served for the creation of plans regarding execution, detailing, costs, and scheduling, while prototypes were made and material experiments conducted at the same time. In the fourth and final phase, the students realized their joint design by carrying out the conversion of the container. It took them only 18 weeks from design to completion of the project.

SBA

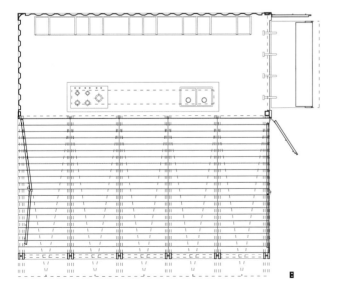

8

5 | Kitchen on the Run in Hof

6, 7 | Axonometric representation of terrace structure

8 | Floor plan of container with assembled terrace

9 | Cooking together in the container

9

Interview

with Rabea Haß and Jule Schröder, founders of Kitchen on the Run, Munich, 24 September 2019
The interview for the TUM Architecture Museum was conducted by Vera Simone Bader and Sina Brückner-Amin.

Had you heard about earlier DesignBuild projects that inspired you? If yes, which ones?
Haß: Not really, at least not under that name. My brother is an architect and works at TUM. He took part in a similar project as a student and helped us to come up with the idea of converting the container together with students.

Schröder: I met an architect friend from Berlin and he told me about a project in Weimar called Die Lücke (The Gap). This pop-up restaurant, which was built as part of a master thesis by an architecture student at Bauhaus University, was also inspiring to us.

Students at the Chair of Architectural Design and Construction at TU Berlin developed the kitchen, furniture, and exterior space under the guidance of Donatella Fioretti. How did the idea of working together on this project come about?
Schröder: We simply googled "container architecture and chair Berlin" and Donatella Fioretti's Chair popped up as the first entry of the search results. We contacted the Chair and spoke to Elke Neumann, who was her assistant at the time. She told me that the topic planned for the next winter semester was "places for cooking and meals." When we first met Donatella and her team at the TU, it took only 20 minutes until we were right in the middle of the planning process of a DesignBuild project. It was immediately clear that we wanted to work together.

What did you expect from the students? What were your specifications?
Schröder: We were quite undiscerning and actually only told them what we planned to do with the space. Our brief fit on a single page: communal cooking, meals at a large table with 20 to 25 people, should be cozy, and convey a homely feeling for one evening. The container was specified as far as space was concerned and also the budget – everything else emerged in the course of the process, such as all the things that had to fit in the shelves.

Did you have a say in the design process? If so, to what extent?
Schröder: We were frequently invited to the interim presentations and inspected the designs together with Donatella Fioretti and her team. The students involved paired up and came up with a total of nine designs focusing on different key aspects. Some concentrated on the furniture, some on how to cover the terrace and some on the design of the fitted kitchen elements. We were involved in the decision-making regarding which of these ideas were finally selected.

Does the design meet your requirements?
Haß: Totally. We were absolutely amazed and felt that the space had great energy right away. Sitting on the wooden terrace with the students for some pizza and beer on the evening before the official inauguration – the tables and benches were still in the workshop for final finishing, the shelf wasn't built yet – we already knew that everyone felt good here. The room was completely finished only one hour before the inauguration in early March, and the gray winter weather made the inviting warmth radiating from our container kitchen all the more evident.

How did the design fare in practice?
Haß: The fact that the container is still so robust and functional is really surprising. We had actually only intended to use it for a half-year tour of Europe. But since the project was – and still is – so successful, people with or without a migration background will be invited to cook together in the container for the fifth year now in 2020. In the meantime, it has been in 17 locations in five countries, at least 7,000 people have cooked inside it, had washing-up parties, have eaten and danced, and it's still in good condition on the whole. In our opinion, "Big Bluey" is our most important team member. The container welcomes you with open arms, and everybody comes, curious and attracted by its beauty. It looks great everywhere – by the sea, in green surroundings, or in a little marketplace.

Has your project changed your view of DesignBuild projects?
Schröder: We didn't have any clear idea of DesignBuild before. Now we would say that simply letting students get on with it is a great idea. Better still if they are supervised as well as they were in our case, by Professor Fioretti's team: with plenty of freedom, but also high standards, requiring them to rethink their ideas and bring them to perfection. The DesignBuild project was an ideal solution for us. Both sides benefitted greatly from the collaboration with the students.

Streetlight Tacloban

LEYTE, PHILIPPINES　　　**NORWEGIAN ARTISTIC RESEARCH PROGRAM (NARP)**

Function: Study center
Size: 100 m²
Building material: Wood, bamboo, concrete

Research phase: 08.2010–12.2010
Planning phase: 08.2010–12.2010
Building phase: 12.2010–05.2011 (destroyed in 2013 and rebuilt in Tagpuro)

Students: 3
Further participants on construction site: 15 parents
Lecturers: Self-organized

Client: Streetlight
Cost: approx. $ 8,160
Financed by: Donations collected by the students, Norwegian architects, Streetlight

Project initiated and led by: Alexander Eriksson Furunes, Trond Hegvold, Ivar K. V. Tutturen (Norwegian University of Science and Technology)

1| Desk space in the gallery

2| Workshop with parents

3| Erection of a roof girder

4| Interior with facade open towards the water

The city of Tacloban is situated in Cancabato Bay on the Philippine island of Leyte. Though an emerging urban metropolis, poverty is still part of everyday urban life in this area, which is one of the world's economically weakest regions. Perhaps this is why the Philippine tradition of bayanihan, a historical form of mutual support that was originally prevalent among the rural communities, is still strong here today. The three architecture students Alexander Eriksson Furunes, Trond Hegvold, and Ivar Tutturen from Norway became familiar with this tradition when they initiated a study center in Tacloban in collaboration with the local NGO Streetlight in 2010. The new center was intended for families of the surrounding informal settlement, providing healthcare, childcare, and a home for children living on the street. During the design process, those in charge adopted the principle of "help for self-help". Together with the children and their parents, the architects developed the project step by step in a series of workshops, with one of the primary planning goals being to transform community values into the built architecture. The architectural process presented a platform for a mutual exchange of knowledge. While the children's mothers took over the determination of the spatial program and design of the study center's three planned buildings during the conception phase, the fathers focused on the realization of the first building, which was completed in the following year. In the course of further workshops, members of the community designed and built furniture and furnishing items, using locally available

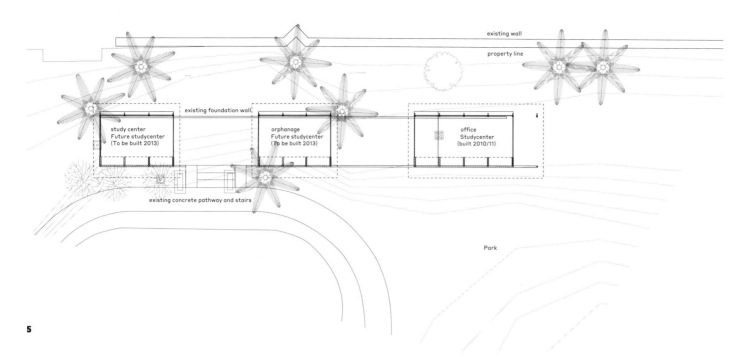

existing wall

property line

Ocean

existing foundation wall

study center
Future studycenter
(To be built 2013)

orphanage
Future studycenter
(To be built 2013)

office
Studycenter
(built 2010/11)

existing concrete pathway and stairs

Park

5

wood. The wood used for the construction of the building was also sourced from a local timber business. An old wall discovered on site ultimately determined the final position of the building. The walls and doors were crafted from bamboo using a traditional technique that had proved itself in the tropical climate with rough winds.

On 8 November 2013, the port city turned out to be one of the most dangerous places in the world, when typhoon Haiyan, one of the most powerful tropical cyclones until then, killed thousands of people and destroyed the city almost entirely. After the catastrophe, the city government decided to relocate the settlements 16 km further northwards along the coast, to Tagpuro. The resettlement strongly impacted the feeling of togetherness in the community, who had no influence on the political decision. In order to provide them with a communal place in the new location, the study center was rebuilt in collaboration with local residents, both adults and children. One of the former students, Alexander Eriksson Furunes, who had in the meantime set up an architectural office, managed to win the community's trust and was invited once again to create the framework for a successful cooperation. He brought along the Philippine architect Sudarshan Khadka. The participants developed a joint idea in over 100 workshops. Drawings, models, and prototypes were used to discuss and try out different solutions for the required uses, spatial orientation, and proportioning of public and private spaces. Children expressed what windows and doors meant to them

through drawings and poems; their parents used these as references for their designs and tested different materials. After determination of the spatial program, the architects concentrated on construction-related matters. The chosen building method was purposely kept simple, so that the local community would be able to master the whole project with their own resources. After three years of intense discussion and planning work, the lost rooms had been reconstructed for the community. According to Eriksson Furunes and Khadka, such an approach to architecture differs from typical project planning in terms of a stronger integration of the local culture, values, and knowledge – a communal resource that forms the basis of a community. The classical planning, conception, design, and construction phases were reinterpreted to allow for participation of the future users, with the participants' shared vision being the main focus of the planning efforts.

EM

5 | Site plan with
planned buildings

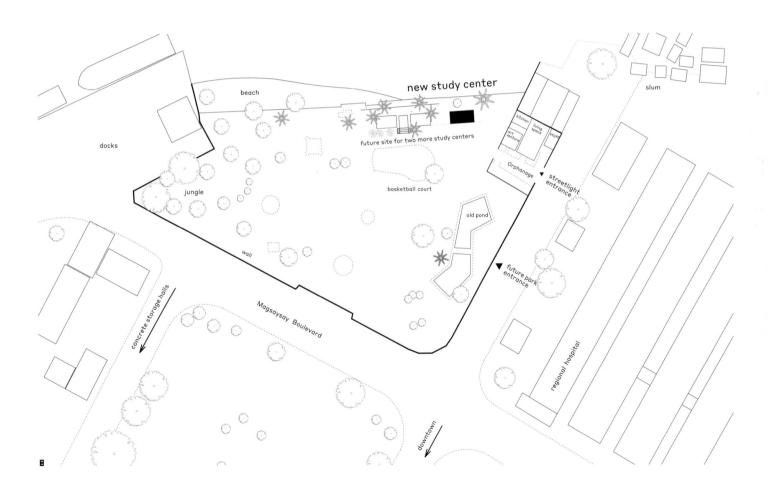

6 | **Entrance of study center**

7 | **Study center, built on existing wall**

8 | **Site and area map**

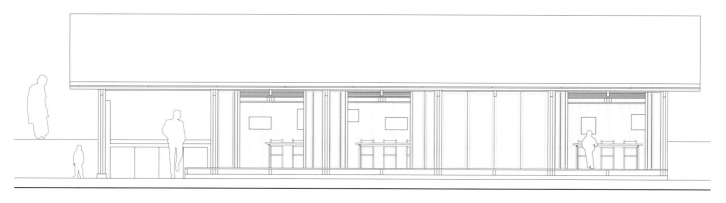

9

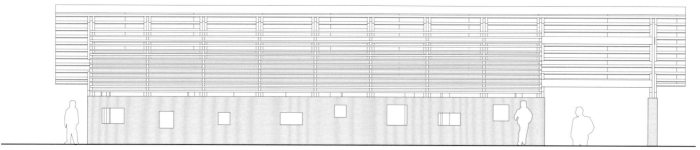

10

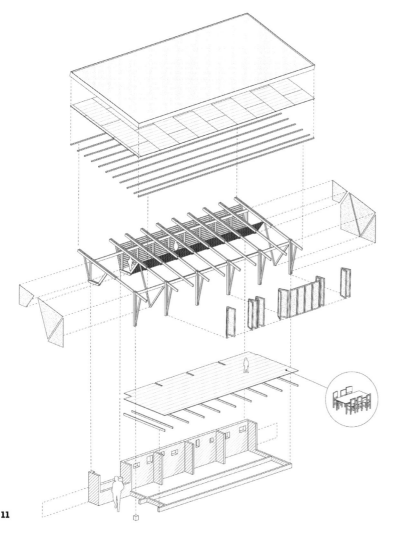

11

12

13

9 | South elevation

10 | North elevation from water

11 | Cross-section of study center

12 | Study center destroyed by typhoon Haiyan

13 | During typhoon Haiyan

14 | Group work on floor plan for new center (Tagpuro)

15 | Group model building (Tagpuro)

16 | Group designing (Tagpuro)

17 | Workshops for new center in Tagpuro

18 | Group specification of spatial program (Tagpuro)

19 | Windows and doors made of wood and bamboo (Tagpuro)

20 | View of center through orphanage (Tagpuro)

21 | Interior of orphanage (Tagpuro)

22 | View of complex

Hospital in Ngaoubela

TIBATI, CAMEROON

TECHNICAL UNIVERSITY OF MUNICH

Function: 1st project: Operating building; **2nd project:** Accommodations for relatives, intensive care ward, and entrance area
Size: 300 m² (operating building), 280 m² (accommodations), 130 m² (hospital entrance/waiting area), 230 m² (emergency room/intensive care ward)

Building material: 1st project: Cement stones, mahogany, loam-straw mixture; **2nd project:** Panel materials (intensive care conversion); cement stones, mahogany (entrance building); loam bricks (adobe), mahogany (accomodations)

Research phase: 09.2011–07.2012
Design phase: 1st project: 10.2011–07.2012;
2nd project: 10.2015–07.2016
Building phase: 1st project: 08.2012–09.2012 (completion 2013);
2nd project: 08.2016–09.2016 (completion 2017/2018)

Students: 20 (design), 8 (execution planning), 8 (building site, per project/design)
Further participants on construction site: 20–30 local workers
Lecturers: 1st project: 2; 2nd project: 4

Client: Hôpital Protestant Ngaoubela, Entwicklungspartnerschaft für Kamerun (Development Partnership for Cameroon)
Cost: EUR 170,000
Financed by: Entwicklungspartnerschaft für Kamerun

Project initiated by: Entwicklungspartnerschaft für Kamerun
Project led by: 1st project: Stefan Krötsch, Matthias Kestel (TUM);
2nd project: Matthias Kestel, Elke Kirst, Christoph Perl, Michael Mayer (TUM)

1 | Erection of a roof girder

2 | View of the completed operating building

3 | Street life with market in Ngaoubela

The Ngaoubela Hospital building ensemble is composed of individual single-story buildings, partly originating from the 1960s. This organically grown conglomeration, however, is deficient in the organization of its spatial sequences, making conversions and extensions difficult. The hospital, supported by an association called Entwicklungspartnerschaft für Kamerun (Development Partnership for Cameroon), which is based in the Vorarlberg region of Austria, has been managed by an Austrian doctor, Elisabeth Neier, since the early 1980s. The association contacted the Technical University of Munich (TUM) with regard to the new construction of a surgical ward in 2010. In the winter semester 2011/2012, students at the Chair of Architectural Design and Timber Construction created a detailed plan for the operating building. They also developed a master plan for future extensions on the entire hospital grounds – including accommodations for family caregivers, an intensive care ward, and an entrance area. The most important challenge for the students was to create a design for a user group with a different cultural background, while at the same time fulfilling the demanding task of building a hospital. Specifications included the creation of a building with a high architectural standard, using a climate-optimized construction methods and saving resources by using biogenic and locally available building materials. Planning and execution of the detailed joining of the building elements had to be simple, well thought-out, and robust, in order to ensure simple maintenance.

The east-west orientation of the long structure of the operating building minimizes solar radiation through open facade areas. Projecting roofs in the north and south provide constant shading of the window surfaces. Wall and support structures were made of locally produced concrete stones. A timber frame construction carries a sheet-metal shed roof

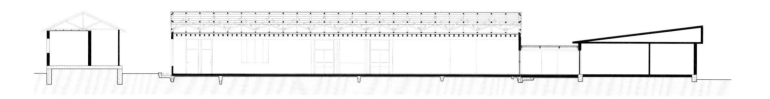

4

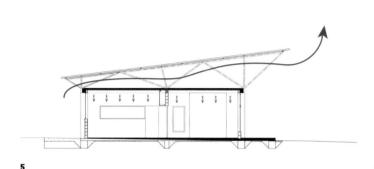

5

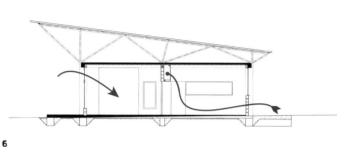

6

above a ceiling construction made of loam pugging. The chimney effect in the space between ceiling and shed roof prevents overheating of the interior. This is supported by a ventilation system especially developed for every facade element. While all the windows in the building have fixed glazing, ventilation takes place via a robust three-level filtering system. The wooden slats of the outer layer keep wind and rain at bay. This is followed by insect netting, which filters coarse suspended particles and insects, while a textile-covered frame prevents dust from entering the interior. All the materials were available at the local market. Exhaust air is removed from the two operating rooms using a pipe system with simple fans.

The operating rooms are located in the center of the right half of the building, with adjoining surgical material handling rooms. The the left side is designed as an open area used to prepare for surgery and includes an anaesthetic recovery room and a staff common room.

Four years later, a second group of students was tasked with building accommodations for relatives of the patients. Relatives looking after patient requirements such as food, drink, and personal hygiene used to sleep under the beds and in the corridors, which interfered with the operation of the hospital. The arrangement of the houses made of air-dried loam stones is reminiscent of the open structures of African villages and provides the relatives with the necessary private space. Meals can be prepared in closed loam ovens in a communal house, rather than on open fires as before.

At the same time, the former surgical wing was converted to an intensive care unit and emergency room. In order to create a large, light-flooded space that was easy to maintain for the intensive care staff, the team broke down almost all of the interior walls. The patient beds are now arranged around a central piece of furniture that not only forms the backbone for medical equipment, but also shortens the span of the supporting structure. Based on the principle of a double roof, the existing shed roof was climatically optimized by means of ventilation openings. A new entrance building with a central reception and waiting area for patients and relatives was completed during the second building phase.

SBA

4 | Longitudinal section of operating building

5 | Climate concept: double roof

6 | Climate concept: natural air supply and mechanical exhaust air

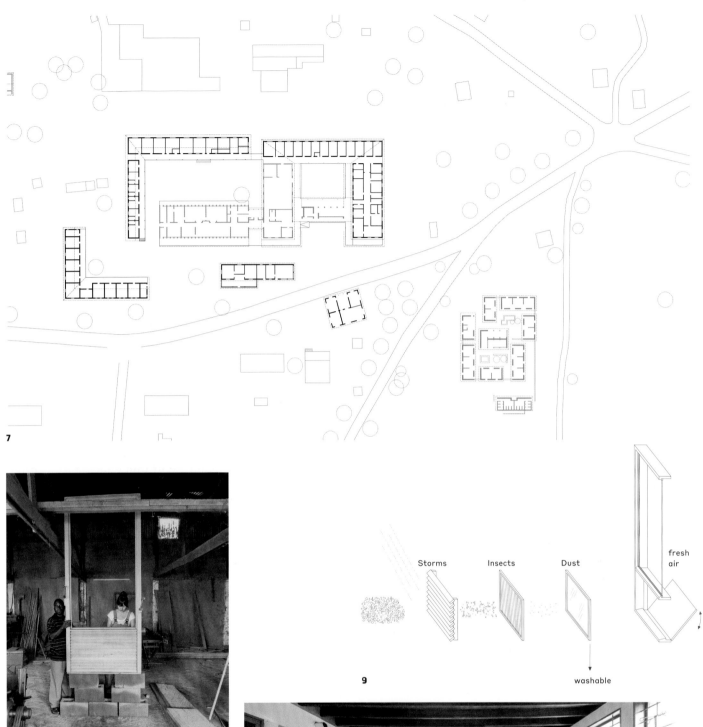

7

8

9

Storms   Insects   Dust   fresh air

washable

10

7 | Site plan of the hospital (operating building, intensive care ward, entrance area and family accommodations)

8 | Fabrication of facade elements with filters

9 | Structure of windows with different filters

10 | Operating room in use

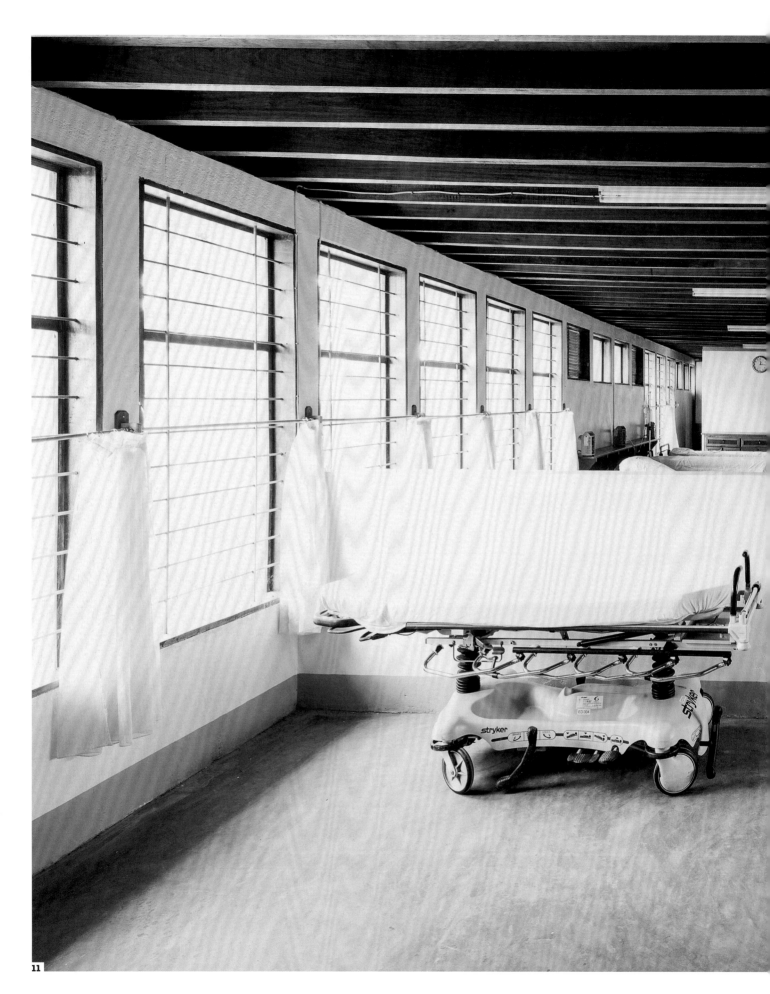

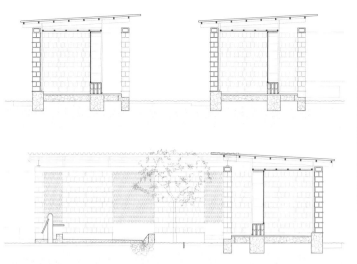

12

13

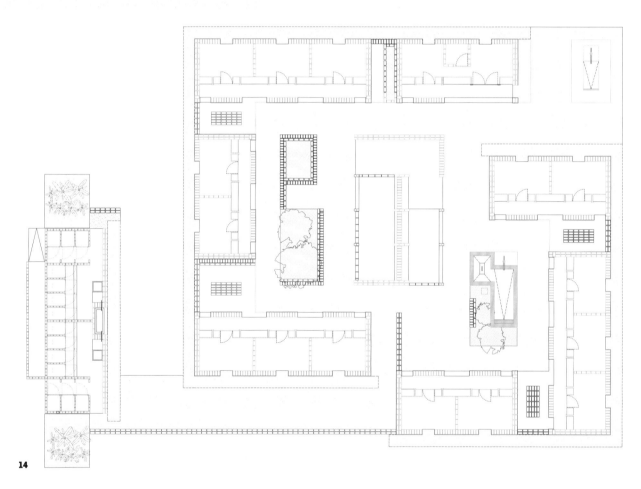

14

15

16

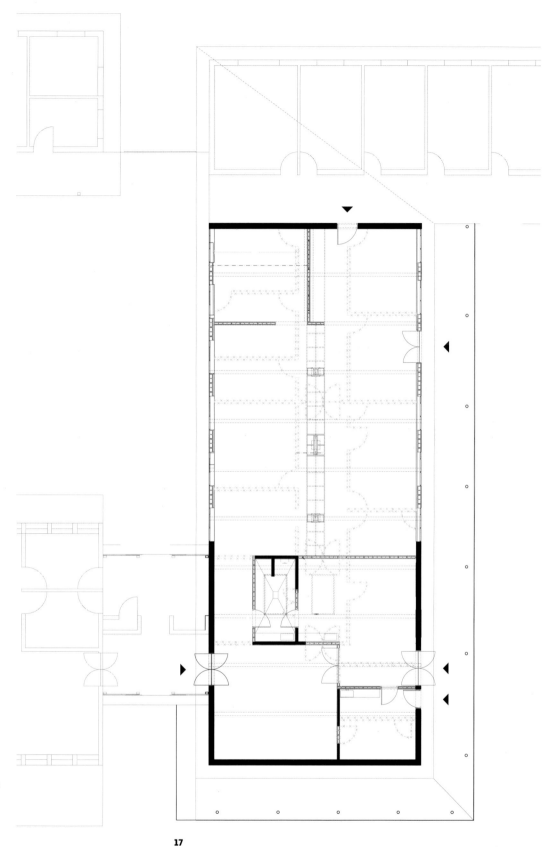

11 | View into the
completed operating
building

12 | Sections of
accommodations for
relatives

13 | Finished buildings
serving to accommodate
relatives

14 | Floor plan of
accommodations for
relatives

15 | Planing wooden
slats

16 | Wooden strips in
window elements

17 | Old (yellow)
and new (red) floor
plan illustrating the
conversion of intensive
care ward

17

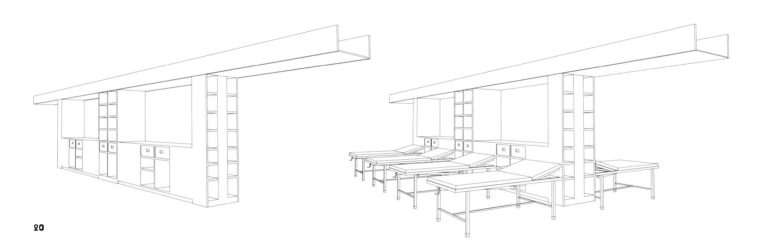

18 | Conversion of intensive care ward

19 | Intensive care ward after conversion

20 | Perspectives of furnishing of intensive care ward

Interview

with Gerhard Müller, Vice Chairman of the association Entwicklungs-partnerschaft für Kamerun (Development Partnership for Cameroon), Munich, 20.09.2019
The interview for TUM Architecture Museum was conducted by Vera Simone Bader and Sina Brückner-Amin.

You are the Vice Chairman of the Development Partnership for Cameroon, which supports the hospital in Ngaoubela. To which extent were you involved in the project?
Müller: The association decided to take on the task of supporting the hospital in Ngaoubela/Tibati. Operated by the Evangelical Lutheran Church of Cameroon, the hospital has been under the medical direction of Dr. Elisabeth Neier from the Vorarlberg region in Austria for 30 years now. As a representative of the association, it was my job to communicate with Prof. Hermann Kaufmann, his assistant Matthias Kestel, and the students [editor's note: all at the Chair of Architectural Design and Timber Construction, TUM], i.e. to raise our ideas and wishes in the regular meetings and to support the development and execution of the project.

Did you also work as a doctor in the hospital in Ngaoubela?
Müller: I am a surgeon and have worked in the hospital a number of times since 2008 – with even greater pleasure in the new operating building.

Has the architecture proved itself in the daily operation of the hospital?
Müller: Yes, of course. The hospital was originally founded as a leprosy ward by Norwegian missionaries. The first buildings were erected over 60 years ago. The old operating ward and the so-called intensive care ward were very basic even by African standards and in a very poor state. The new operating room building is not only attractive and functional, but has a generous layout and hence future possibilities, should the hospital be expanded. The large roof of the new operating building was astounding at first, because of its size, but the underlying ventilation concept is brilliant and works well.

How do the patients find the new building?
Müller: The expectations of the patients themselves aren't that high. But the new buildings make a significant contribution to improving medical care. We also hoped to attract doctors from other parts of Cameroon with the improved infrastructure and such a nice operating area, because Ngaoubela is rather remote and not very tempting. But so far, we have only had limited success.

What demands did the association and specifically the doctors make on the project?
Müller: The association approached the TUM primarily with the request to design an easily built and cost-effective building that would function well under the specific local conditions and significantly improve the operating area. The old operating ward was to be converted to an intensive care ward in a second step. Such an intensive care facility cannot be compared to one in Germany, it mainly provides space for good post-operative care and monitoring of seriously ill patients.

Why did you approach the TUM?
Müller: Originally, the intention was to have the project exclusively handled by the hospital operator and African firms. We would however have had very little influence on the design in this case. And we also didn't have the essential contacts. An important member of our association, Dr. Alois Lang, also a doctor, has known Prof. Hermann Kaufmann for a very long time. That's how the opportunity to work together with the TUM came about.

How did you find the collaboration with the students?
Müller: Really good. It certainly was a lengthy process, since the project was also a teaching assignment. The basic preparation phase was therefore fairly time-consuming. But this allowed us to bring in our ideas very well.

Looking back, are there any points about the project that you would criticize or do you have any suggestions for improvement?
Müller: Not really. The only criticism that I can think of is the time limitation. The problem came up when the accommodations for relatives was built. This could only be done during the European summer holidays, which was the rainy season in Cameroon. It would have been a lot easier to build in the dry season. The time structure of the course, however, did not allow this. A recommendation for improvement would therefore be to change the time frame a little in order to be able to take local weather conditions into consideration.

DesignBuild projects are often accused of focusing too much on materials and neglecting architectural quality in the process, while also fostering neocolonial structures. What do you make of that?
Müller: In the case of our project, we did in fact primarily set down the fundamental plans according to our views, in conjunction with Dr. Neier. One could perhaps call this "imposed on". We do however believe that we are very familiar with the local situation and the requirements of the hospital. Prof. Hermann Kaufmann also traveled to Cameroon with us and we discussed the plans there on location together with relevant representatives of the hospital staff. One of these discussion partners was also the medical director of the Evangelical Lutheran Church of Cameroon. All the wishes and ideas voiced there were included in the plans. Another significant factor was that Dr. Neier, who has gained high renown far beyond Ngaoubela through her 30 years of work in the hospital, was involved in the project right from the start. African firms and workers played an important part in the realization of the project. This made it possible to acquire all the materials locally and to integrate local structures effectively. The design of the accommodations for relatives was purposely kept very simple and built using adobe. This turned out to be a problem since loam structures – although still common in local residential building – are considered inferior in rural Africa. The "old" adobe method is regarded as outdated, while bricks and concrete are viewed as better and preferable building materials. Considerable persuasive efforts were therefore necessary, which finally proved to be successful also because, thanks to technical details, improved resistance to weathering of the buildings could be achieved. This can also be considered an inspiration and model for the local population to go back to using more economical and resource-friendly loam for their own houses.

| BUILD

Pou Pir Elementary School

BATTAMBANG PROVINCE, CAMBODIA

FACULTY OF DESIGN, SHIH CHIEN UNIVERSITY, TAIPEI (USC); FLYOUNG INTERNATIONAL SERVICE OF TAIPEI MEDICAL UNIVERSITY (TMU)

Function: Healthcare area, classroom, library, drinking water supply, hand-washing area
Size: 6 m x 16 m
Building material: Concrete, wood

Research phase: 02.2019–06.2019
Planning phase: 06.2019
Building phase: 06.2019–07.2019

Students: 18
Further participants on construction site: 3–10
Lecturers: 3

Client: Pou Pir Elementary School
Cost: $ 8,000 (building), $ 3,000 (drinking water supply)
Financing: 60% Ministry of Education of Taiwan, 30% private sponsors, 10% Shih Chien University Taipei

Project initiated and led by: Gou-Chou Chen (USC), Gina Gou (TMU)

1 | Working on the timber construction

2 | New building and existing school building

3 | Setting up the timber construction

Active in Cambodia since 2013, Shih Chien University Taipei (USC) has built healthcare areas, classrooms and toilets that were urgently needed there. The university cooperated with the FLYoung International Service of Taipei Medical University (TMU), which has also been active in Cambodia for years, for the project in Pou Pir in 2019. The village of Pou Pir consists of about 100 stilt houses and is located in the Province of Battambang in the northwest of Cambodia. The FLYoung International Service not only established contact to the community and existing elementary schools, but also defined part of the building task: a drinking water supply as well as an area for healthcare were to be created. Since the lack of classrooms was also a major problem, the students of the USC proposed the inclusion of an open classroom in the plan as well as adding an optional library to the design.

In the spring semester of 2019, ten students of the USC received instruction in the traditional timber construction methods used by the Chinese, the Japanese, and the Khmer in the studio of Associate Professor Gou-Chou Chen. They were also familiarized with the types of wood that could be considered for the building work and learned how to use the materials for construction. Individually created designs gave the students a deeper understanding of the project. At the end of the semester, the students erected a full-size wooden pavilion on the USC campus in just eight hours. The steps required for this – from design, listing all the required types of wood, developing structures, to realization – were to

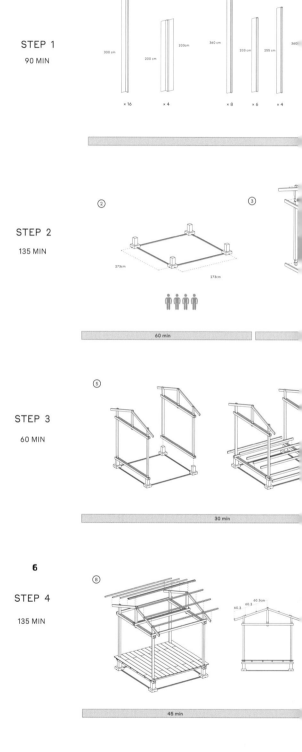

give them a first insight into the work method that was expected of them two weeks later on site in Cambodia. The 18 students who traveled to Pou Pir were split into four teams. Each of the teams was headed by two or three of the eight students who had prepared for the project in the spring semester. After studying the building site, the teams worked out and presented a design in compliance with the building task, all on the first day. Two out of four of the proposals were chosen, revised, and presented again for selection of the final design. This was a timber construction built on stilts, based on the building style used by the Khmer, which the team leaders had been familiarized with during the spring semester. The next morning, the students worked on a material list and bought the required timber at the local market in the afternoon. The following eight days were dedicated to building concrete pillars to carry the timber construction, connecting the beams to form a supporting structure on the ground outdoors, and erecting it. This was followed by cladding the floor, the walls, and the roof, which is additionally held by iron rods. The villagers assisted the students with the building work, with communication facilitated by an interpreter or articulated non-verbally.

STEP 1
90 MIN

STEP 2
135 MIN

STEP 3
60 MIN

6

STEP 4
135 MIN

4 + 5 | Wooden pavilion
on USC campus

6 | Time schedule
for construction of the
wooden pavilion

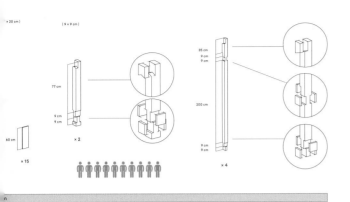

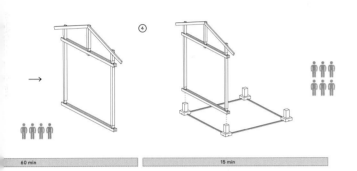

7 hours / 10 people

×10   ×12   ×5   ×2
×2   ×2   ×2

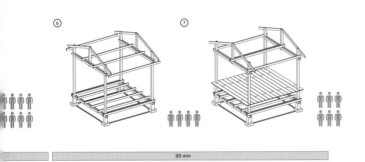

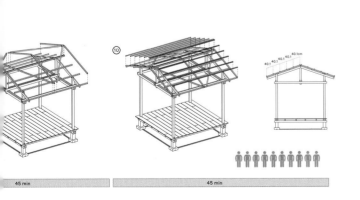

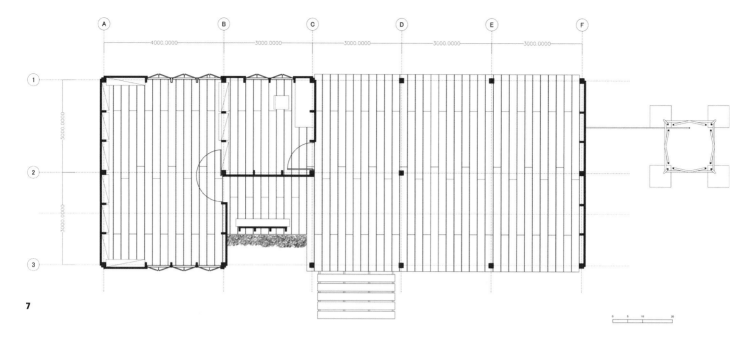

7

This resulted in a construction with central wooden stairs, leading to an open space that allows a view of the pond opposite covered with lotus blossoms. It serves as a transition to the open classroom on the one side as well as to the healthcare area with library on the other side. The new building is situated opposite to an already existing school building. This has resulted in a clear definition of the space in between, creating a small campus. Outside the building is an additional installation comprising a water hose and taps. The children can take water to drink from there. The building was put into service soon after its completion.

The FLYoung International Service realized its part of the building task – the drinking water supply – together with students of the TMU. Pupils had previously brought unfiltered drinking water from home and fetched water from the nearby pond to clean the toilets. The students built a water tower, comprising – from top to bottom – three tanks with a volume of 1,000, 500 and 2,000 liters. Groundwater is pumped into the 1,000-liter tank from a fountain. This serves for storage and the necessary pressure on the 500-liter tank, which contains biosand for filtration of the water. The filtered water is then transferred to the 2,000-liter tank, and from there, to the water pipes. Unfiltered water from the 1,000-liter tank is used directly for hand washing and toilet flushing.

VSB

7 | Floor plan of new construction and water tower

8 | Cutting the wooden beams to length

9

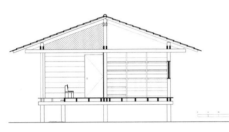

10

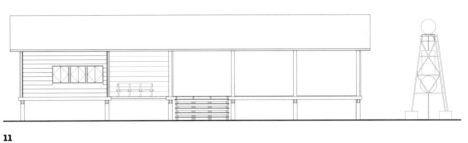

11

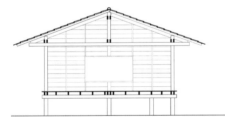

12

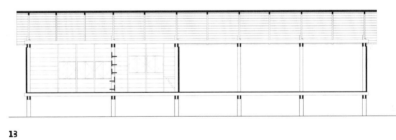

13

14

15

9 | New building with water tower

10 | Cross-section of library room

11 | Elevation of new building with water tower

12 | Cross-section of open classroom

13 | Longitudinal section of new building

14 | Drinking water system

15 | Toilet facility of school

1

2

OBENauf in Unternalb

RETZ, AUSTRIA

DESIGN.BUILD STUDIO, TECHNICAL UNIVERSITY OF VIENNA

Function: Bed-and-breakfast facility
Size: 950 m²
Building material: Concrete, birch plywood, solid Douglas fir

Research phase: 10.2014
Planning phase: 11.2014–01.2015
Building phase: 03.2015–02.2016

Students: 25
Further participants on construction site: 8 employees of the sheltered Caritas workshops, 1–5 employees of the construction company, as well as local specialized companies (electrical, heating, plumbing, carpentry)
Lecturers: 1

Client: Caritas Vienna
Cost: not stated
Financed by: Caritas Vienna

Project initiated by: Markus Zoller (Head of Building Department of Caritas of Archdiocese Vienna & Lower Austria-East)
Project led by: Peter Fattinger (design.build studio, TU Vienna)

1 | **Building site of conversion**

2 | **Reception of new hotel**

3 | **Existing building in backyard**

Unternalb Farm is located on a former farm estate of Göttweig Abbey in Unternalb in the Lower Austrian municipality of Retz. Since 1984, it has been run by Caritas Vienna as an institution for people with disabilities, providing an opportunity for training and employment in the field of organic farming as well as in various workshops. A vacant side wing of the historical farm estate presented an opportunity to extend the workshops in terms of space and program. The wing was to be converted into an accommodation facility and subsequently run as a bed-and-breakfast by the people with disabilities. In 2014, the Design-Build studio of TU Vienna, which had already carried out a variety of construction projects with and for the Caritas in the past, was invited to develop an appropriate architectural concept for the structural alteration with its students, followed by realization in collaboration with local specialized companies and the people with disabilities working in the farm estate's Caritas workshops.

Building within existing stock poses a challenge for a DesignBuild project, especially in a listed building like the farm estate in Unternalb. It limits the design scope while opening up other areas of work. The Federal Monuments Authority Austria (BDA) was already involved during the first on-site design workshop in autumn 2014 and continued to support the entire process. Only very rough plans of the existing structures were available, which meant that the students had to start by taking measurements. They used a laser scanner provided by a construction software company to accurately record the geometry of the

4

arched rooms. The property had also been subjected to various alterations and installations, starting in the middle of the previous century. The deconstruction of these was the first building activity by the students and the people with disabilities. Over a period of almost three months, plasterboard walls and suspended ceilings were dismantled, walled-up corridors and windows were reopened, wood and stone floors removed, numbered and temporarily stored, the ground floor soil was dug out to the depth of a meter to facilitate the installation of an appropriate insulation below ground level, and a dilapidated outbuilding was demolished. In the course of the dismantling work, a historical ceiling fresco was found under a suspended ceiling, which was entrusted to a restorer. The students' design mainly focused on alterations

and installations in the interior space, as well as on the conversion of the backyard. Five guest rooms for a total of ten persons and a common room were created on the upper floor of the existing two-story building, which has a floor space of around 350 m². A ceiling height of nearly 4.50 m permitted sanitary facilities to be installed in the rooms in the form of boxes with a height of 2.30 m.

Niches with a clothes rail, shelf, and desk were fitted on the outer wall of the boxes. Also integrated in the wall of the sanitary boxes is a staircase leading to a gallery that can be used as a place to retreat or as additional sleeping space.

The rooms on the ground floor are characterized by vaulted ceilings. Adjacent to the reception, which also functions as a farm shop, is a breakfast room with a

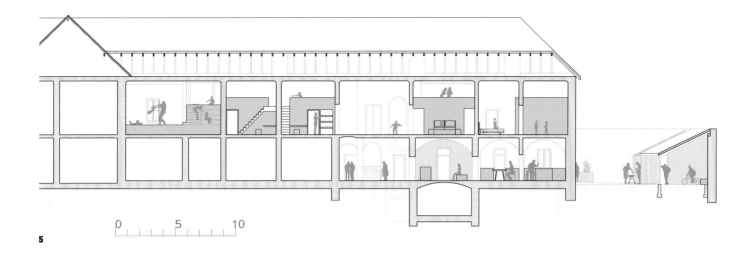

5

large table and a kitchen that is available on request to guests in the evening. Meals can be prepared on a 5-meter-long kitchen counter cast out of high-performance concrete by the students.

The design of the backyard also formed part of the project. A dilapidated outbuilding was demolished and replaced by a new construction of exposed concrete that serves as a protected seating area, storage room, and bike shed. Raised beds for planting, a barbecue area, and seating in the courtyard were also made from cast, exposed concrete by the students. To enable barrier-free access, an annex in the courtyard was gutted and fitted with an elevator.

Since completion in spring 2016, OBENauf has been closely involved in the running of Unternalb Farm and the guest rooms are booked as accommodation for tourists. The people with disabilities working in the hotel and hospitality trade gain valuable work experience there, which is intended to help them to find employment on the labor market later.

SBA

6

4 | Site plan of bed-and-breakfast

5 | Longitudinal section with new installations marked green

6 | Main building from inner courtyard

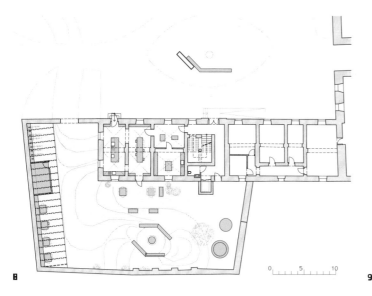

8

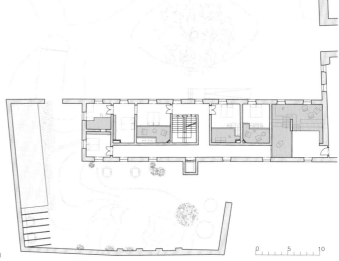

9

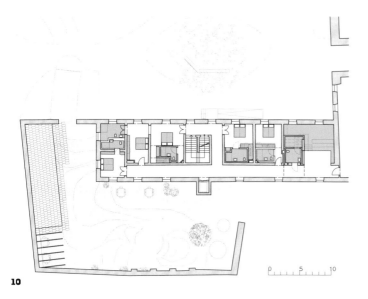

10

13

11

12

14

7 | View of the complex
from the courtyard

8 | Floor plan of ground
floor, with changes
marked green

9 | Floor plan of gallery
floor, with changes
marked green

10 | Floor plan of upper
story, with changes
marked green

11 | Installation of
intermediate ceiling

12 +13 | Guest room

14 | Breakfast room

Interview

with Thomas Krottendorfer, Caritas Regional Director for People with Disabilities in the Weinviertel Region, Unternalb, 23 September 2019
The interview for TUM Architecture Museum was conducted by Vera Simone Bader.

The building project OBENauf in Unternalb was realized by the Caritas in conjunction with the DesignBuild studio of TU Vienna. How did this collaboration come about?

The Caritas branch of the Archdiocese of Vienna already had experience in working together with TU Vienna. That's how it came to the proposal by the building department for another project in Unternalb. We found our first discussion with Prof. Peter Fattinger [editor's note: Director of DesignBuild studio at TU Vienna] in early 2014 very convincing.

What specifications did you make on your part?

We naturally attach great importance to the involvement of our clients. We had gone through an ideation process before, which is where the idea of a bed-and-breakfast in place in the Unternalb farm originated. In 2013, the building in which OBENauf is now located became available. We shared many of the results of this process with Prof. Fattinger: coming together in the sense of inclusion was very important to us. We wanted to have communal areas created for this. Important criteria included functional and suitable work areas for people with disabilities, as well as accessibility – an architecturally attractive and affordable conversion of the monastic building in the Retzer Land was what we aimed for. Guests should feel a little changed when they leave, and the architecture is very helpful in this regard.

What were your requirements from the students?

To start with, we presented our work, our guiding principles, and our approach. The participation of our clients was a prerequisite, and something that was practiced and taken into consideration in an outstanding manner throughout the process. We enjoyed experimenting together and that also left us enough time for planning. Starting from an enthusiastic idea, the way everything turned out – including finding a logo and a name – is something we are very grateful for.

Why did you consider the DesignBuild method suitable for the Caritas project?

The form and culture of working together was a good fit for us: putting oneself in someone else's position and trying to understand them, acting with sensitivity and empathy, and producing and accepting a diversity of opinions. We were invited often and regularly during the design process. During the creative phase, there was so much on the table that offered ample opportunities for collaborative decision-making. It was just the right pace for our work. And finally, it was important for us to have a contact partner in the form of such a team right from the start all the way to the handover of the keys – in the design, realization, and even advertising phase.

How did the collaboration with the students work out?

I believe that the project was mutually challenging and rewarding in a way that also changed us: on our part, with regard to issues such as historical preservation, architecture, and difficult building tasks; on the students' part it was working with people with disabilities. Our guiding themes "I can do it" and "A disabled person is disabled by others" surely had a positive influence on the project. An interest in, a sensitivity for, and a response to the topics of each respective partner was what connected us.

Does the architecture satisfy your requirements?

The fact that they extend across multiple stories makes the rooms more cosy while optimally utilizing the space, but also endows them with a unique feature. Communal areas in the inner courtyard and the upper floor show that our wishes were taken seriously – also in the breakfast room, through the shared table. Adopting the tile pattern in the logo was such a great idea. The Goldene Kelle [editor's note: a distinction for exemplary building design in Lower Austria, awarded by the magazine GESTALTE(N)] or the repeated booking.com awards confirm our feeling that we managed to create something really good here.

What could work better next time?

Maybe more clarity regarding who makes which decisions and takes on which tasks. Our shared enthusiasm led to an energetic and inspiring start, and responsibilities became clear only after a while – both on the side of Caritas and that of the students. At the same time, I consider this to have been of great benefit, because we managed to create clarity together. Perhaps I would also involve the neighborhood in the common themes more – as the charity organization that we are, we took on a lot of this, because we consider cooperation in the region to be very important. If we had held such talks together beforehand, the project may have profited from some fine tuning. I don't regard this critically, but rather as an opportunity for future projects.

Library in Newbern

HALE COUNTY, ALABAMA, USA

RURAL STUDIO, AUBURN UNIVERSITY

Function: Library
Size: 182 m² (library), 590 m² (yard, parking spaces)
Building material: Wood, original bricks

Research phase: 08.2012–12.2012
Planning phase: 11.2012–08.2013
Construction phase: 05.2013–05.2015

Students: 4
Lecturers: 3

Client: Newbern Library Board
Cost: not specified
Financed by: not specified

Project initiated and led by: Rural Studio, Newbern;
Newbern Library Board

1 | Breakthrough of
existing wall

2 | Finished library

3 | Transition from
already existing building
to new construction

As one of the oldest DesignBuild initiatives, Rural Studio has been active in western Alabama for more than 25 years. Rural Studio is linked to Auburn University and situated in Newbern, Hale County, in the so-called Black Belt of Alabama. Its projects are financed entirely by donations, while the university covers the administrative costs. The donors support architectural projects with a direct positive impact on the living conditions in Hale County, an in many ways undersupplied area, primarily due to social components: people move away due to lack of employment, there are only few schools and administration departments have been relocated to the next larger city. Vacancy is therefore not uncommon in Newbern. The bank building, constructed on the main road of the city in 1906, had also been unused for some time when a group of residents got together in Hale County in 2012 and expressed their wish to have a community center. Their idea was that a library would lend itself particularly well to combining aspects of social interaction and education and they assigned Rural Studio with the reconstruction of the bank building.

What role does a library play in the present and how can it be realized within a historical building in need of rehabilitation? These were the questions addressed by the students and the Rural Studio team during the planning phase. Since the project was part of the current curriculum of Rural Studio, planning and construction had to be completed within eight months. The students used research trips to regional city libraries to help them to work out a concept for

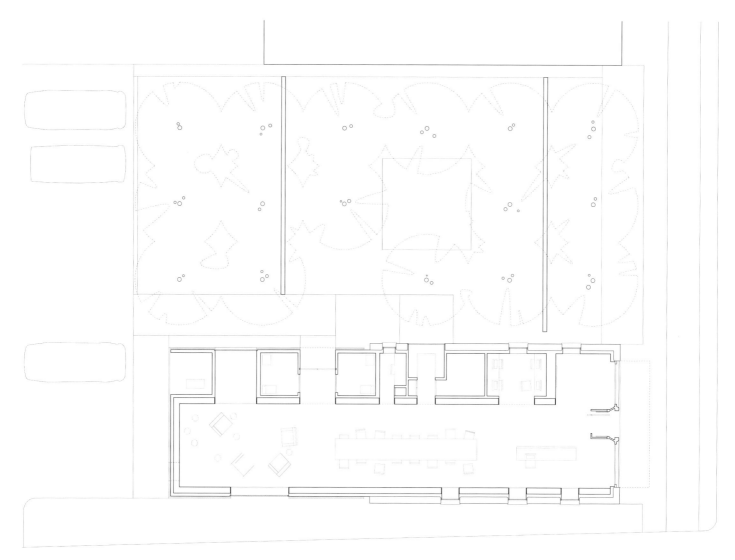

4

the new library. A fundamental feature of the design is the architectural extension, which comes out of the back of the building like a drawer, while leaving the characteristic facade unchanged. The interior space was divided in a longitudinal direction, with a series of niches formed in the right half that can be accessed from the open, left half of the reading room. In addition to a storeroom and sanitary facilities, there are four individual reading tables for solitary or group work. A seating corner and a newly fitted window offer a special place for retreat, with views of the green courtyard that was paved by the students using previously removed bricks.

The remodelling process started with the gutting of the historical building. The students dismantled the modules by hand to avoid damaging the more than 100-year-old carpentry work of the interior partition walls. The same applied to the pinewood floor. The project was then ready for the rough building work. This involved breaking down the rear wall of the building as well as excavation of the damp soil, which was then recast along with the base plate for the extension. Next followed the interior finishing work

with the wooden construction joining the historical part and the extension to form a continuous interior space. Essential measures to keep library costs at a minimum and to protect the books from moisture include the new interior design as well as a multilayer spray foam-based insulation.

While the outside walls of the bank building were restored and the former windows merely exchanged to preserve the aesthetics, the extension with its wood panelling is a tribute to the horizontally structured brickwork, yet clearly distinguished through the irregular distribution and sizing of the windows. These were designed and crafted in collaboration with Zane Morgan and Cassandra Kellogg from Rural Studio and fitted in the masonry by the students. In contrast to the historical wooden windows, they have a thin steel frame and look as though they have been punched into the facade.

While the exterior construction clearly reveals the differences between old and new, the interior space offered an opportunity to create a sense of seamless space. The continuous bookshelves made from birch plywood panels were created by the students

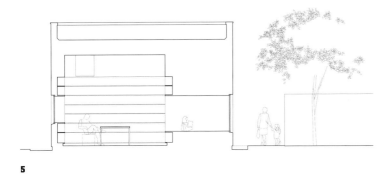

5

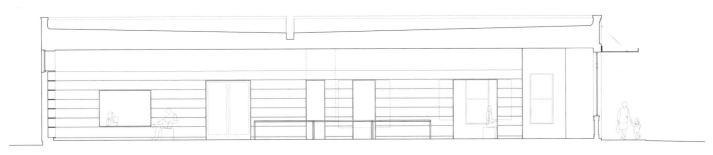

6

7

4 | Floor plan of library
with inner courtyard

5 | Cross-section of
library

6 | Longitudinal section
of library

7 | Timber frame system
of new construction

8 | Exploded axonometric
view of roof structure

8

in a multistage process with renderings and mock-ups — the final conclusion being that it was virtually impossible to build the shelves to fit accurately by hand. Therefore, they braved the gap and turned the visible tolerance gaps between the shelves and the access doors into a design element. Refurbished pinewood planks were used to clad walls and floors, while partition walls were converted into a reception desk and reading table. Historical and contemporary materials are combined on new and surprising levels in this design.

SBA

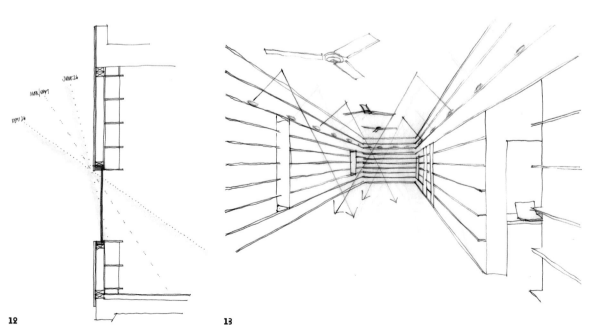

9 | Deconstruction of old interior furnishing

10 | Model of design

11 | Sketches of design

12 | Study on incidence of sunlight

13 | Study of indirect, artificial lighting

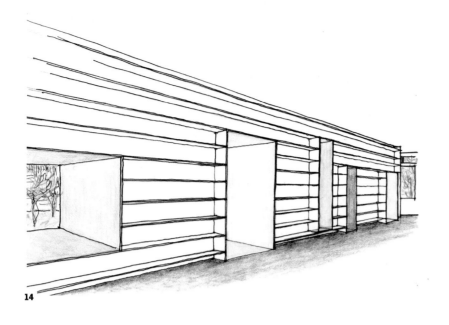

14 | Perspective drawing of interior

15 | Installation of shelves

16 | View of inner courtyard through new window

17 | Interior of library with visible lighting

18 | Paving with bricks from the original building

19 | Green inner courtyard

THANKS

Both the exhibition and catalogue Experience in Action! DesignBuild in Architecture would not have been possible without the help and support of many colleagues, friends, and staff working in Germany and abroad.

Above all, our thanks go to the Sto Foundation, represented by Uwe Koos, Chairman of the Foundation Council, whose generous financial support made the exhibition and catalogue possible in the first place.

Special thanks also go to the Hans Sauer Foundation, in particular to the CEO of the foundation, Ralph Boch, for his help in getting the Kitchen on the Run project to Munich.

We would further like to express our gratitude to PIN. Freunde der Pinakothek der Moderne, and Arte Generali for their support so that the DesignBuild Pavilion could be built outside the museum during the exhibition.

Our personal thanks go to:

Attila Acs, Antoinette Aichele-Platen, Ferdinand Albrecht, Siegfried Atteneder, Dietlind Bachmeier, Bernd Bader, Jakob Bahret, Katrin Bäumler, Tomà Berlanda, Marlies Blasl, Andreas Bohman, Alejandro Borrachia, Anna-Maria Brendel, Helena Brückner, Sina Brückner-Amin, Lorena Burbano, Shpresa Cekaj, Gou-Chou Chen, Peter Cheret, Teddy Cruz, Marc Drewes, Martin Düchs, Teresa Fankhänel, Peter Fattinger, Enrica Ferrucci, Donatella Fioretti, Nils Fischer, Konstantin Flöhl, Fonna Forman, Clara Frey, Alexander Furunes, Susanne Gampfer, Verena Gerlach, Yasmin Gründing, Mengxue Guo, Ursula Hartig, Rabea Haß, Bernadette Heiermann, Anton Heine, Martina Heinemann, Adam Hopfner, Laura Höpfner, Carola Jacob-Ritz, Michael Jany, Elisabeth Judmaier, Verena Karasek, Hermann Kaufmann, Mira Keipke, Matthias Kestel, Moritz Klein, Franz Klein-Wiele, Eglė Kliučinskaitė, Jakob Köppel, Tonderai Koschke, Stefan Krötsch, Thomas Krottendorfer, Anupama Kundoo, Christophe Leik, Nico Lewin, Leoni Lichtblau, Thomas Lohmaier, Martin Luce, Elena Markus, Anna-Maria Meister, Rike Menacher, Sarah Meyer, Martin Mitterhofer, Gerhard Müller, Florian Nagler, Benny Nast, Katharina Neubauer, Claire Nicholas, Pia Nürnberger, Arlene Oak, Franziska Odametey, Sebastian Oviedo, Yasemin Özdemir, Philipp Paeslack, Sergio Palleroni, Ralf Pasel, Jazek Poralla, Judith Reitz, Jaime Reyes, Christoph Rokitta, Juan Román, Thomas Georg Schaplik, Vincent Sebastian Schmitt, Jule Schröder, Christian Schühle, Frederick Schunemann, Thilo Schuster, Ulrike Schwantner, Spela Setzen, Roswitha Siegler, Hans Skotte, Stella Sommer, Ansgar Stadler, Nicola Stadler, Christian Stahl, Benedikt Stoib, Antal Strausz, Hilde Strobl, Laura Traub, Konstantin Trautmann, Maximilian v. Sporschill, Lukas Vallentin, Xavier Vendrell, Hermann Verkerk, Alessandro Visentin, Tanja Vollmer, Dorothee Wahl, Felix Waldner, Heide Wessely, Stefan Widdess, Barbara Wolf, Alain Yimbou, Keith Zawistowski, Marie Zawistowski, Lennard Zimmermann.

PHOTO CREDITS

P. 8, 9, 172 above, 173, 175 below, 176, 177, 178 above right, 180 above left and above right © Matthias Kestel

P. 10 Collection of Masato Nakagawa, Gift of Mary Emma Harris, Black Mountain College Project © Western Regional Archives, State Archives of North Carolina

P. 12 © M.h.De. Source: Hannes Meyer, Wikipedia (https://fr. wikipedia.org/wiki/Hannes_Meyer)

P. 13 Beaumont Newhall © Beaumont and Nancy Newhall Estate. Source: Black Mountain College, Wikipedia (https://de.wikipedia.org/wiki/Black_Mountain_College)

P. 15, 18, 19 © Archivio Historico José Vial

P. 20 © Vadim Zakharov. Source: Theodor W. Adorno, Wikipedia (https://de.wikipedia.org/wiki/Theodor_W._Adorno)

P. 23 © Henning Scharf

P. 28, 29 © Florian Haydn

P. 30, 130 left, 132 below left, 132 below right © Paulina Ojeda

P. 32, 62, 166, 167, 168, 169 below, 170 above, 170 below left, 171 © Alexander Eriksson Furunes

P. 33, 140 left, 141, 142 above, 143, above, 143 below left © DesignbuildLAB, Grenoble School of Architecture (ENSAG)

P. 34 © Sherry Arnstein. Source: Sherry Arnstein, Wikipedia (https://en.wikipedia.org/wiki/Sherry_Arnstein)

P. 36, 148, 149, 150, 151, 152 above, 152 middle, 152 below right, 153 below, 154, 155 © RWTH Aachen University/PBSA University of Applied Sciences Dusseldorf/ Georgia Institute of Technology School of Architecture

P. 38, 39 © Red Bull Amaphiko

P. 40 left © Maxi Rottenwalk

P. 40 right, 41, 42 © Atarraya Taller de Arquitectura

P. 44, 45 © Santiago Oviedo

P. 46, 48, 49, 50, 51, 52, 53 © Max Waske

P. 47 © Helena Brückner

P. 54, 58, 59 © Ursula Hartig

P. 56, 57 © Studio Chamanga, Munich University of Applied Sciences

P. 60 Andreas Rost © CODE, Technical University of Berlin

P. 64 © Hans Skotte

P. 65, 67 © Lael Aprieto

P. 68, 70, 71 © Timothy Hursley

P. 72, 74 Gemma Koppen © Kopvol Architecture and Psychology

P. 78, 79 © Javier Callejas

P. 80, 82, 83 © Arlene Oak

P. 86, 87 © Kristin Solhaug Nœss

P. 88, 90, 92, 93, 95, 97 © Estudio Teddy Cruz + Fonna Forman

P. 98, 126, 127, 128, 129 © Center for Public Interest Design (CPID), Portland State University

P. 100, 102, 103, 104 © Gustavo Burgos © University of Talca

P. 106, 107 Benny Nast © Labor Fou

P. 108, 109 right, 112, 113 © Kurt Hörbst

P. 108 above; 109 left: Dominik Abbrederis © BASEhabitat, University of Art and Design Linz

P. 110 left © BASEhabitat, University of Art and Design Linz

P. 110 right, 206, 207 © Stephanie Hüber

P. 111, 114 right; 115, 116 right; 117 © Flavia Matei, Max Weidacher, BASEhabitat, University of Art and Design Linz

P. 114 left, 116 left © Sebastian Vilanek

P. 118, 119, 121 © CODE, Technical University of Berlin

P. 120 © Jade University of Applied Sciences

P. 122, 123, 124, 125 © IRGE, University of Stuttgart

P. 130 right, 131, 132 above, 133 © Studio Quiané, Munich University of Applied Sciences

P. 134 left, 135, 138 middle © Atelier U20

P. 134 right, 136, 137, 139 below © Yannick Wegner

P. 138 above © Sandra Gressung

P. 138 below © Viktor Poteschkin

P. 139 above © Tobias Vogel

P. 140 right, 142 below, 143 below right © Eduard Hueber

P. 144, 145, 146, 147 © FADAU, University of Morón

P. 152 below left, 153 above, 153 above © Wieland Gleich

P. 156 left, 158, 159 above, 159 middle, 159 below left © Yale School of Architecture

P. 156 right, 157, 159 below right © Zelig Fok and Iain Gomez

P. 160, 162, 163 © Lêmrich

P. 161 © Christoph Rokitta

P. 164 above, 164 below left © FG Fioretti, Technical University of Berlin

P. 164 below right © Frank Seibert

P. 169 above © Nelson Petilla

P. 170 below above right, 170 below right © Streetlight

P. 172 left, P. 175 above left © Susanne Steinmaßl

P. 174, 175 above, 175 above right, 178 above left, 178 middle, 178 below, 179, 180 below © TUM DesignBuild, Technical University of Munich

P. 182, 183, 184, 185, 186, 187 © Shih Chien University

P. 188 left, 189, 190, 191 above, 194 above, 194 above left, 194 below left © design. build studio, Vienna University of Technology

P. 188 right, 194 middle right, 194 below middle and right © Markus Fattinger

P. 191 below, 192, 193 © Peter Fattinger

P. 196, 197, 198, 199, 200, 201 © Rural Studio, Auburn University

STUDENT PARTICIPANTS

Sunderpur Housing
BASEHABITAT, UNIVERSITY OF ART AND DESIGN LINZ

Hinda Bouabdallah, Yoann Cormerais, Hana Davidkova, Paul Eis, Sophie Haselhofer, Vincent Hirrien, Benedikt Hofmann, Valentina Hölzl, Su-Mara Kainz, Yuti Kainz, Cornelia Kriechbaumer, Olivia Kudlich, Mathilde Leibfried, Lucia Mackova, Diego Martinez, Flavia Matei, Ana Melnicenco, Vittoria Mittelstädt, Eva Neumayerova, Julien Reinhart, Anne Maren Rotter, Eva Schmolmüller, Lea Stahnke, Jasmin Steinberg, Marlena Unterberger, Maria Wächter, Lavinia Wagner, Vinzent Wallner, Max Weicher, Francesca Zanella

Co-Housing Oldenburg / Home not Shelter!
TECHNICAL UNIVERSITY BERLIN; JADE UNIVERSITY OF APPLIED SCIENCES OLDENBURG

Domenic Degner, Natalya Dikhanov, Ilkim Er, Julian Franke, Andreas Hauthal, Agnes Helming, Liska Hinrichs, Arne Köller, Heba Kolodziej, Stefan Neumaier, Florian Tropp

Centro Comunal Alto Perú
E1NSZUE1NS, UNIVERSITY OF STUTTGART

Cynthia Aguirre, Moritz Berg, Fatima Castro, Leonie Ederer, Valerie Franck, , Martin Feustel, Martin Gonzales, Eider Yarrizu Inoriza, Kristina Kolb, Alexandra Larrea, Flavia Milachay, Susanne Pardo, Joselyn Salinas, Miguel Santivanez, Yannik Schröder, Jialing Wang, Marija Zivanovic, Mariana Zollino

Experimental (Re-)construction and Northern Cheyenne Resilience
CENTER FOR PUBLIC INTEREST DESIGN, PORTLAND UNIVERSITY

Zeljka Asmait, Tim Barnette, Natasha Broman, Lauren Chamberlain, Willy Chandler, Cameron Davis, Valeria Degutis, Galen Dominic, Molly Esteve, Todd Ferry, Loren Gillingham, Therese Graf, Lee Huer, Marteen Jiménez, Thomas Jones, Tomasz Low, Julia Mollner, Hailey Nelke, An Nguyen, Brandon Parker, Alejandra Ruiz, Matt Rusnac, Grayson Schoenbine, Shannon Smith, Yuki Takemura, Stephanie Vance, Emily Waldinger, Reid Weber, Haley Wilson, Joseph Wilson, James Zoeller

Quiané DesignBuild Studio
MUNICH UNIVERSITY OF APPLIED SCIENCES

Konrad Baron, Konstantin Bauer, Lorena Burbano, Raphael Caizergues , Maria Jose Chiriboga Ramirez, Alexander Goncalves da Silva, Ferdinand Hecht, Lisa Holzapfel, Anna Viktoria Kozma, Marinus Kurz, André Matulla, Jhony Morales, Olga Petrenko, Dorothea Rader, Iván Ramirez, Thomas Reiner, Néstor Reyes, Alejandro Rodriguez, Maximilian Rottenwaller, Philippe Sauer, Philipp Streit, Florian Stuffer, Merlin Tichy, Johanna Weise, Hannah Wiesenfeld, Melis Yücesan

Community Center Spinelli
TECHNICAL UNIVERSITY KAISERSLAUTERN

Johannes Ackermann, Soheyl Aslani, Sandra Gressung, Sonja Hiegle, Annika Koch, Alina Kohl, Tobias Kohlstruck, Bei Liu, Konrad Peter, Viktor Poteschkin, Sascha Ritschel, Arved Sartorius, Manuel Scheib, Nicolas Treitz, Tobias Vogel, Lukas Weber, Lu Yuan, Ying Zhang

Maison pour tous (House for All)
DESIGN/BUILDLAB, ENSAG – GRENOBLE SCHOOL OF ARCHITECTURE:

William Audin, Magda Audrerie, Roderic Archambault, Wafa Benjarmoun, Salomé Bergsma, Petronille Blondon, Matthieu Bo, Hugo Boulanger, Louis Bouret, Alice Cavallasca, Clémence Drouard, Laurence Lebel, Louise Mary, Lucas Munoz, Margaux Regalia, Louise Renault, Raphaelle Ruiz, Esméralda Tabai, LinhVu Thuy, Laura Tinas, Clément Venton, Héloise Viola

STUDENT HOUSING
FACULTY OF ARCHITECTURE, DESIGN, ART AND URBANISM, FADAU, UNIVERSITY OF MORÓN

Cristian Alvarez, Veronica Brautigam, Lucas Guerra, Leandro Iannaci, Jose Lagues Caballero, Leandro Pinheiro, Florencia Tomalino, Marcia Velazquez

Guga S'Thebe Theater
**PBSA, DÜSSELDORF HSD
RWTH, AACHEN
GEORGIA TECH, ATLANTA
CS STUDIO ARCHITECTS, CAPE TOWN
IMAGINE STRUCTURE, FRANKFURT A.M./COLOGNE**

Chaye Agbetou, Tim Andrasko, Whitney Ashley, Kardar Aslan, Miriam Attallah, Ulrike Baumann, Victor Bausinger, David Baxter, Dominique Boh, Paola Both, Katelyn Bouret, Mary Briatta, Ria Briers, Larissa Brüsehafer, David Bulenda, Leo Busch, Nikita Campbell, Christine Cangelosi, Benedict Christensen, Virginia Classen, Markus Claudy, Louis Coetzee, William Collar, Johan Cornelius, Bob Cousseillant, Ali Crownover, Sara Damiani, Cedric Daniels, Levke Danker, Brittney Davis, Amelia Deaton, Tiemo Deller, Hannah Diermann, Qingxian Du, Nadine Duffe, David Duncan, Andile Dyasi, Phoebe Edalatpour, Marie Ehrenstein, Rana Elkholi, Franziska Enderle, Andres Erazo, Max Ernst, Friederike Essfeld, Anne Fabritius, Steffi Faff, Anna Lena Faltin, Elisabeth Faßbender, Hanna Fokken, Kristina Franke, Paula Frasch, Adrian Fuhrich, Smina Gahlen, Jose Garza De La Cruz, Elsa Gaugué, Jeremy Gentry, Dimitri Georgeades, Pitt Lion Gerlich, Lorraine Gerrans, Nele Geßner, Donovan Geysman, Hannah Goldstein, Katja Göser, Valerie Gottburg, Lisa Goubeaux, Cora Hanquet, Natalie Harper, Margot van Heerden, Ashley Hemraj, Friederike Henne, Peter Henshall-Howard, Sarah Hesse, Henning Hessel, Nadia Heyers, Lena Hille, Nico Hillen, Ann-Denise Hinse, Lavinia Hoeck, Erika Hogan, Laura Hohlfeld, Renee Holleman, Conrad Idensee, Louise Ing, Riaan Ismail, Saul Jacobs, Meredith James, Peter Jamieson, Nadja Jung, Pieter Junge, Robin Jutzen, Ashwin Kamath, Norman Kamp, Mareike Kapitza, Katrin Karos, Dilsoz Kasim-Sieto, Amelie Kastrup, Jana Kausemann, Tarik Kaya, Catharina Keckstein, Laure Kerger, Conrad Kersting, Thomas Kersting, Vanessa Kiefert, Daniel Kim, Taylor Kitchens, Lena Klein-Erwig, Fabian Klemp, Thomas Klinkhammer, Peter Koen, Fabian Konkol, Hannah Koschinski, Joana Koslowsky, Inna Kotel, Theresa Kotulla, Jelena Krämer, Michelle Kraus, Annika Krause, Evelyn Kreuzer, Nico Kückemanns, Christian Kühnle, Anna Kuretzky, Mogamat Landers, Quy Le, Gerald Lee, Juliet Leslie, Julia Leucht, Yingcheng Liang,

Eesa Limbada, Daniela Lindner, Paloma Longhi, Theresa Lücke, Mona Makebrand, Elahe Maleki, Jacqueline Mancher, Marco Martens, Nicklette Marques Pires, James McDaniel, Jana Mentges, Dennis Mertens, Dillon Mertens, Jannik Metje, Miriam Metje, Tina Meyer, Bongani Mgijima, Elena Miegel, Andrew Miller, John Miller, Zayd Minty, Sabrina Mix, Leila Moghimi, Ronja Monshausen, David Moore, Xoliswa Morara, Alia Mortada, Khaled Mostafa, Isabelle Motschull, Joana Münster, Landile Mzalisi, Mediha Nazli, Christopher Neuwirth, Ashley Newman, Judith Neyses, Miriam Nguan, Rosa Niggemann, Nils Oehler, Greteakiny Ohlendorf, Morgan Orvino, Takuto Osawa, Carl von Oy, Zehra Özdilek, Janina Pahlke, Kyra Pahlke, Carina Pardun, Lukas Pauw, Pia Aletta Peters, Grey Peterson, Nathalie Pszola, Liu Qiao, Shamila Rahim, Dominique Ramrath, Geoffrey Rees, Jens Renneke, Paul Reynolds, Liessa Riebesel, Henriette Riecke, Matthias Rietze, Joanna Robinson, Felix Röder, Sebastian Rothkopf, Vanessa Rottstädt, Kaleigh Sawyer, Christian S. Schantz, Thomas Schaplik, Lukas Schlüter, Anna Schneider, Cornelia Schneider, Kristin Schoening, Daniel Schröder, Maike Schulz, Nicolas Schulz, Carolin Schulze, Tina Schumann, Julia Schwippe, Andreas Seegmüller, Juliane Seehawer, Gregory September, David Serna, Wang Shu Wu, Renate Sibgatullina, Robert Siebrits, Craig Sissing, Kay Sommer, Anne Sonnefeld, Dennis Sonntag, Simon Spenrath, Shona Stali, Nikolija Stamenkovic, Magdalena Stephan, Ancunel Steyn, Laura Stock, Matthias Stromberg, Brian Sudduth, Samila Sydiq, Phebe Tam, Brian Tarrant, Sarah Tendler, Günay Terzi, Marina Thelen, Kara Thomas, Abraham Venter, Pascal Völz, Johannes Walterbusch, Luise Watolla, Berit Wenthaus, Svenja Wenzel, Fiona Westphal, Constantin Wiemer, Tim Winter, Anne Worpenberg, Austin Wright, Di Wu, , Ru Yang, Ebru Yazici, Derin Yilmaz, WenWen Zhao

2019 Jim Vlock Building Project
YALE SCHOOL OF ARCHITECTURE, YALE UNIVERSITY

Ife Adepegba, Isa Akerfeldt-Howard, Natalie Broton, Ives Brown, Chris Cambio, Martin Carrillo Bueno, Colin Chudyk, Jiachen Deng, Janet Dong, Xuefeng Du, Paul Freudenburg, Kate Fritz, Malcom Galang, Anjelica S. Gallegos, Kevin Gao, Ian Gu, Jiaming Gu, Ashton Harrell, Liang Hu, Niema Jafari, Alicia Jones, Hyun Jae Jung, Sze Wai Justin Kong, Louis Koushouris, Tyler Krebs, Hiuku Lam, Pabi Lee, Isabel Li, Mingxi Li, Dreama Lin, April Liu, Qiyuan Liu, Araceli Lopez, Angela Lufkin, Rachel Mulder, Leanne Nagata, Naomi Ng, Alex Olivier, Louisa Nolte, Michelle Qu, Nicole Ratajczak, Scott Simpson, Heather Schneider, Christine Song, Shikha Thakali, Ben Thompson, I-Ting Tsai, Sarah Weiss, Max Wirsing, Stella Xu, Shelby Wright, Sean Yang, Peng Ye, Leyi Zhang, Yuhan Zhang, Kevin Zhao, Sasha Zwiebel

Kitchen on the Run
TECHNICAL UNIVERSITY OF BERLIN

Michaela Apfel, Philine Barbe, Sophia Braun, Ammon Budde, Theodora Constantin, Marcel Hecker, Lya Kröger, David Leinen, Jonathan Lewkowicz, Juri Lux, David Potthast, Benjamin Schaad, Judith Schiebel, Stefan Schöllhammer, Anton Sieber, Nico Sonnenbrodt, Corinna Studier, Vanessa Vogel, Jonas von der Wall

Streetlight Tacloban
NORWEGIAN ARTISTIC RESEARCH PROGRAM (NARP)

Alexander Eriksson, Furunes, Trond Hegvold, Ivar K. V. Tutturen

Hospital in Ngaoubela
TECHNICAL UNIVERSITY OF MUNICH

Hanna Albrecht, Franziska Berkíc, Doria Bornheimer, Lotta Ewert, Julia Graeff, Nina Kleber, Karina Knüchtel, Sophie Kotter, Michael Mayer, Vinzenz Mayer, Leonie Morano, Jonas Pauli, Magdalena Pfeffer, David Stanzel, Stephanie Tröndlin-Ehrler, Phillip Weibhauser

Pour Pir Elementary School
FACULTY OF DESIGN, SHIH CHIEN UNIVERSITY, TAIPEI (USC); FLYOUNG INTERNATIONAL SERVICE OF TAIPEI MEDICAL UNIVERSITY (TMU)

歐陽羽童. U-Tong Ao Leong, 陳旻薇. Min-Wei Chen, 鄭晴予. Ching-Yu Cheng, 丘郁茹. 江恆瑞. Heng Jui Chiang, Yu-Ju Chiu, 朱德芸. Te-Yun Chu, 解晉軒. Chin-Hsuan Hsieh, 許峻韶. Jyun-Shah Hsu, 許力云. Li-Yun Hsu, 許敬柔. Ching-Jou Hsu, 黃蕙靜. Yi-Jing Huang, 黃博暄. Po-Hsuan Huang, 李承睿. Cheng Rui Lee, 李宜臻. Yi-Chen Lee, 李共. Kong Lee, 李雪濤. Xue-Tao Li, 林孟樺. Meng-Hua, Lin, 盧國聰. Kuok-Chong Lou, 蘇奕恒. I-Heng Su, 吳偉新. Wei-Shin Wu, 游治豪. Chih-Hao Yu, 游俊庭. Chun-Ting Yu

OBENauf in Unternalb
DESIGN.BUILD STUDIO, TECHNICAL UNIVERSITY OF VIENNA

Susanne Baume, Jan Felix Enzlberger, Hannah Ertel, Lea Furbach, Martina Soi Gunelas, Benedikt Hanser, Max Hofmann, Doris Holzapfel, Lisa Jochum, Roswitha Kranzinger, Raphaela Leu, Johanna Maria Lindinger-Pesendorfer, Laura Lipensky, Flavia Iulia Matei, Maximilian Ostermann, Sebastian Pernegger, Caroline Pflügl, Nina Pongratz, Florian Seiringer, Benjamin Softic, Raphael Stocker, Daniela Stöger, Johanna Maria Waldhör, Raphael Wenzl, Ahmet Zu

Library in Newbern
RURAL STUDIO, AUBURN UNIVERSITY,

Morgan Acino, Ashley Clark, Stephen Durham, Will Gregory

▶ **Construction site in Sunderpur, construction of the residential building, which mainly consists of clay and bamboo. DesignBuild project "Sunderpur Housing", Bihar, India, Linz Art University, 2017**

This book was published on the occasion the exhibition
EXPERIENCE IN ACTION!
DESIGNBUILD IN ARCHITECTURE
at the Architecture Museum of the Technical University of Munich at the Pinakothek der Moderne:
19 March to 14 June 2020

Funded by

Sto Foundation

PIN. Friends of the Pinakothek der Moderne, Arte Generali

EXHIBITION

Director: Andres Lepik
Curator: Vera Simone Bader
Research fellow: Jakob Bahret
Assistants: Clara Frey, Laura Höpfner, Mira Keipke, Eglé Kliucinskaité, Stella Sommer, Alessandro Visentin, Lennard Zimmermann
Exhibition design: Labor Fou und Event Architectuur
Graphic design: Milkmonkey
Videography & editing: Michael Jany
Interview partners: Sigfried Atteneder, Konstantin Bauer, Helena Brückner, Lorena Burbano, Shpresa Cekaj, Maria Jose Chiriboga Ramirez, Tatjana Dürr, Andreas Emminger, Susanne Gampfer, Ursula Hartig, Ferdinand Hecht, Lisa Holzapfel, Moritz Klein, Viktoria Kozma, Stefan Krötsch, Sebastián Oviedo, Martin Mitterhofer, Franziska Odametey, Ralf Pasel, Merlin Tichy
Exhibition installation: Andreas Bohmann, Thomas Lohmaier, Anton Heine
Registrar: Thilo Schuster
Proofreading: Carola Jacob-Ritz, Stefan Widdess
Image editing: Esther Vletsos
Administration: Marlies Blasl, Tina Heinemann, Rike Menacher, Tanja Nyc

CATALOGUE

Editors: Vera Simone Bader, Andres Lepik
Chief editor: Vera Simone Bader
Editorial assistants: Jakob Bahret, Sina Brückner-Armin, Barbara Wolf
Translation into English: Yasmin Gründing
Copyediting: Stefan Widdess, Alisa Kotmair
Graphic Design: Verena Gerlach
Project texts: Vera Simone Bader (VSB), Sina Brückner-Amin (SBA), Teresa Fankhänel (FT), Elena Markus (EM)
© 2020, first edition
Architekturmuseum der TUM and DETAIL Business Information GmbH
Messerschmittstrasse 4
80992 Munich
detail.de

ISBN 978-3-95553-514-8

Project manager: Heide Wessely
Editor-in-chief: Dr. Sandra Hofmeister
Production DTP: Roswitha Siegler
Proofreading: Alisa Kotmair
Reprographics: ludwig:media, Zell am See
Printing and binding: Kösel GmbH & Co. KG, Altusried-Krugzell
Paper: Profibulk 135 g
Cover: Peyprint glatt 130 g

The German National Library lists this publication in the the German National Bibliography. Detailed bibliographical data can be found at: http://dnb.d-nb.de.

Cover: Design for the Yale School of Architecture's Jim Vlock First Year Building Project, photo: © Yale School of Architecture